（汉英对照版）

# 一 杯 茶

[英] 曼殊斐尔　著　　　徐志摩　译

辽宁人民出版社

# A CUP OF TEA

by Katherine Mansfield
Translated by Xu Zhimo

Ⓛ Liaoning People's Publishing House

**图书在版编目（CIP）数据**

一杯茶 /（英）曼殊斐尔著；徐志摩译. —沈阳：辽宁人民出版社，2017.1（2020.6重印）

（小经典译丛）

ISBN 978-7-205-08646-6

Ⅰ.①一… Ⅱ.①曼…②徐… Ⅲ.①短篇小说—小说集—英国—现代 Ⅳ.①I561.45

中国版本图书馆CIP数据核字（2016）第166502号

出版发行：辽宁人民出版社
　　　　　地址：沈阳市和平区十一纬路25号　邮编：110003
　　　　　电话：024-23284321（邮　购）　024-23284324（发行部）
　　　　　传真：024-23284191（发行部）　024-23284304（办公室）
　　　　　http://www.lnpph.com.cn
印　　刷：山东华立印务有限公司
幅面尺寸：110mm×180mm
印　　张：6.5
字　　数：90千字
出版时间：2017年1月第1版
印刷时间：2020年6月第2次印刷
责任编辑：刘国阳
封面设计：展　志
版式设计：姿　兰
责任校对：耿　珺等
书　　号：ISBN 978-7-205-08646-6

定　　价：20.00元

# 出版说明

纵观中外翻译史，翻译活动与语言的发展密不可分。英语发展的各个重要阶段，翻译都发挥了重要作用，不仅丰富了英语的词汇，又极大地增强了英语的表现力。反观我国，古代的佛经翻译对汉语的用词、句法等均产生了影响。胡适的《白话文学史》中讲到，"维祇难，竺法护，鸠摩罗什诸位大师用朴实平易的白话文体来翻译佛经，但求易晓，不加藻饰，遂造成一种文学新体"。我国19世纪中叶起有意识地译介西方的地理、历史、政治、法律、教育的书籍，这些翻译活动大大丰富了汉语中的词汇，很多词汇已经融入日常用语并沿用至今，如"文学""法律""政治""铁路""贸易"等。到了19世纪末期和20世纪初期，梁启超所倡导的"新文体"对当时的读书人有着相当大的影响，而所谓"新文体"即是融合了浅近文言、翻译输入新名词、叙述自由、不合"古文义法"的文体。"小经典译丛·民国名家名译"所精选的翻译作品，就是在这样的背景下诞生的。无论是徐志摩还是郁达夫，均是从小耳濡目染着"新文体"同时又接受了良好的文言和外文的教育。因而，他们的译文既融合了本人母语写作的诗化、含蓄、连绵的特点，也将欧化的语言带入译文。从他们的译文中足以管窥汉语白话文推演之一斑。20 世纪 30 年代语言学家钱玄同谈及汉语过渡时期，曾说应"用某一外国文字为国文之补助"；论及所选语种，则谈"照现在中国学校情形而论，似乎英文已成习惯，则用英文可也"。故而当时的一些知识分子也在译介域外文学时自觉地通过翻译来"改造"语言，例如周作人所倡导的"直译"等。无论是顺应西文词序不自觉地翻译，还是对汉语白话有意识地"改造"，使这一时期的作品都彰显了独特的语言气质——自由、含蓄、唯美、诗意，虽然不能妄言达到"信、达、雅"之境，却也力求用最精到的用词和与原文灵魂契合的句式，用独具风韵的白话进行表达。这也在某种程度上为这些名家的母语创作提供了借鉴。从徐志摩和郁达夫等人的现代诗和散文作品中，也能见到这种语言"改造"的影子。

　　尽管在习惯了现代汉语行文的读者看来，这些名家的译文多有机巧、不够平易，甚至有些不通，但如果放在当时的背景之下，就可以客观评价和欣赏这种文风的妙处。另外，民国初期很多地名、人名等尚没有严格的规范译名，尤其在文学翻译里，常见到译者的别具匠心的音译或直译，虽缺少了规范，略有理解障碍，但这种自由也促成了一些精妙的译名诞生，如"翡冷翠"（佛罗伦萨）、"沁芳"（交响乐）这样的灵动传神，恐在今天一定是不合规矩、不合时宜的了。

　　丛书甄选这一时期名家的译介作品，编排名篇的中英文对照，旨在为喜爱欣赏文学和英文的读者提供中英文对照的素材，从比照原文和译文了解名家甄选原文、推敲译文的良苦用心，近距离感受他们的文化底蕴，并从中体会 19 世纪末20 世纪初世界新旧交替、风云激荡的大背景下，中国文人的趣味和心境。阅读这套丛书，不仅可以品读双语文学经典，还可借此回溯语言文化一路发展的长河，于浪涛中取这一杯啜饮。

丛书编辑过程中，尽量保留了译著的原状，借此为读者呈现民国初期珍贵的语言面貌。编辑过程中仅对个别生僻词句加注说明，并对译文的形式略有改动，如删去了《古代的人》原译中的部分英文括注，以避免与原文对照功能重复。由于编选时间仓促、水平有限，一定有很多不足与疏漏之处，敬请读者批评指正。

辽宁人民出版社

# 代　序

　　几个月前，受辽宁人民出版社编辑邀约，为他们精编的一套民国名家经典译丛作序，并收到电子初稿小样。虽执教英文近30年，翻译专业书籍、英美小说、杂文等文字量近200万字，但为学贯中西的大文学家、民国时期精英才俊郁达夫、徐志摩、林徽因等人的译作写序，岂敢？故几番推辞，不敢承约。但手中拥有了这份来自故乡的电子书小样，我如获至宝。在北欧夏日极昼极长的日光里，工作之余，悠闲地坐在斑驳树荫下、湖边草坪上或街边咖啡座里，我先睹为快。捧书细读，重温英汉对译的妙与美，我似乎穿越到了上个世纪二三十年代的民国时期，与我少年时起就崇拜的冷峻的郁达夫、才情的徐志摩和美丽的林徽因在方方正正的中文里相遇啦！我在字里行间感受民国时期那股清新的译风，在诗化的素美语言中玩味彼时翻译的乐趣，徜徉在看似信手拈来却也处处机巧的篇章中，时空仿佛凝滞在那精读时刻。

年少时，也曾读过英文原著小章节。一路走来，人生中年，在英语语境中深入到久远的原著，伴着波罗的海海边的余晖，我再一次理解郁达夫作品《沉沦》与他的译作《幸福的摆》的某种关联。主人公华伦徘徊在理性与感性之间，命运从悲喜转为平和，仿佛那身边大海，时而惊涛拍岸，汹涌澎湃，而后又归于平静安详，不禁抒发感叹：这就是人生啊！

某个晴朗的周末，我在湖边草坪席地而坐，像个12岁的小姑娘般充满好奇地读完了亨德里克·威廉·房龙撰写、林徽因译就的《古代的人》。房龙像个博学的圣诞老人，精巧细致地引领读者走入历史长河，贴切的行文勾画人类进步的面面观。而时年22岁的美丽才女林徽因用她缜密的逻辑、精致的文字、纯熟的译法再现原著风格。读她的作品如同欣赏她设计的精美建筑，那样灵动，那样飘逸。

徐志摩的诗才尽人皆知，他的字句清新、意境优美和神思飘逸，历来是文青们效仿的典范。美慧的英国女作家曼殊斐尔人格的精华给了诗人灵澈，他们惺惺相惜。最适合在一个绵绵细雨的日子，捧一杯咖啡或清茶，读《园会》，品《一杯茶》，看《理想的家庭》之模样。诗人用他如诗般的音律，典雅的人名转译，神奇点睛之笔，重现多位栩栩如生的欧美人物形象，亲切而又陌生，仿佛老上海城隍庙游园会，走来一群曼妙的蔷媚，谈着雨夜的翡冷翠……

　　快生活时代，让我们的思想、思绪慢下来，品读经典，体会文字语言的译介之美。让这译介的"媒"引领我们走入东西方文化的"国际理解"之中吧！


　　　　　　　　　　　　　　　　张东辉

　　　　　　　　　　（英语教授、维尔纽斯大学

　　　　　　　　　　孔子学院中方院长）

　　　　　　　　　　　　　　于维尔纽斯

　　　　　　　　　　　　　　2016年7月

# 目 录

# CONTENTS

# 园　会

　　那天的天气果然是理想的。园会的天气，就是他们预定的，也没有再好的了。没有风，暖和，天上没有云点子。就是蓝天里盖着一层淡金色的雾纱，像是初夏有时的天气。那园丁天亮就起来，剪草，扫地，收拾个干净；草地和那种着小菊花的暗暗的平顶的小花房儿，都闪闪地发亮着。还有那些玫瑰花，她们自个儿真像是懂得，到园会的人们也就只会得赏识玫瑰花儿；这是谁都认得的花儿。好几百，真是好几百，全在一夜里开了出来；那一丛绿绿的全低着头儿，像是天仙来拜会过她们似的。

　　他们早餐还没有吃完，工人们就来安那布篷子。

　　"娘，你看这篷子安在那儿好？"

　　"我的好孩子，用不着问我。今年我是打定主意什么事都交给你们孩子们的了。忘了我是你们的娘。只当我是个请来的贵客就得。"

　　但是梅格总还不能去监督那些工人们。她没有吃早饭就洗了头发，她带着一块青的头巾坐在那里喝咖啡，潮的黑的发卷儿贴在她两边的脸上。玖思，那蝴蝶儿，每天下来总是穿着绸的里裙，披着日本的花衫子。

　　"还是你去吧，老腊；你是讲究美术的。"

　　老腊就飞了出去，手里还拿着她的一块牛油面包。

　　她就爱有了推头到屋子外面吃东西；她又是最爱安排事情的；她总以为她可以比谁都办得稳当些。

　　四个工人，脱了外褂子的，一块儿站在园里的道儿上。他们手里拿着支篷帐的杆子，一卷卷的帆布，背上挂着装工具的大口袋儿。他们的神气很叫人注意的。老腊现在倒怪怨她自己还拿着那片牛油面包，可是又没有地方放，她又不能把它掷了。她脸上有点儿红，她走近他们的时候；可是她装出严厉的，甚至有点儿近视的样子。

　　"早安，"她说，学她娘的口气。但是这一声装得太可怕了，她自己都有点儿难为情，接着她就像个小女孩子口吃着说，"嘎——欧——你们来——是不是为那篷帐？"

"就是您哪，小姐，"身子最高的那个说，一个瘦瘦的，满脸斑点的高个儿，他掀动着他背上的大口袋，把他的草帽望后脑一推，望下来对着她笑。"就是为那个。"

他的笑那样的随便，那样的和气，老腊也就不觉得难为情了。多么好的眼他有的是，小小的，可是那样的深蓝！她现在望着他的同伴，他们也在笑吟吟的。"放心，我们不咬人的。"他们的笑像在那儿说。工人们多么好呀！这早上又是多美呀！可是她不该提起早上，她得办她的公事，那篷帐。

"我说，把它放在那边百合花的草地上，怎么样呢？那边成不成？"

她伸着不拿牛油面包的那只手，点着那百合花的草地。他们转过身去，望着她点的方面。那小胖子扁着他那下嘴唇皮儿，那高个子皱着眉头。

"我瞧不合适，"他说，"看得不够明亮。您瞧，要是一个漫天帐子，"他转身向着老腊，还是他那随便的样子，"您得放着一个地基儿，您一看就会'嘭'地一下打着你的眼，要是您懂我的话。"

这一下可是把老腊蒙住了一阵子，她想不清一个做工的该不该对她说那样的话，"嘭"地一下打着你的眼。她可是很懂得。

"那边网球场的一个基角儿上呢？"她又出主意，"可是音乐队也得占一个基角儿。"

"唔，还有音乐队不是？"又一个工人说。他的脸是青青的。他的眼睛瞄着那网球场，神气看得怪难看的，他在想什么呢？

"就是一个很小的音乐队。"老腊缓缓地说。也许他不会多么地介意，要是音乐队是个小的。但是那高个儿的又打岔了。

"我说，小姐，那个地基儿合适。背着前面那些大树，那边儿，准合适。"

背那些喀拉噶树。可是那些喀拉噶树得让遮住了。它们多么可爱，宽宽的，发亮的叶子，一球球的黄果子。它们像是你想象长在一个荒岛上的大树，高傲的，孤单的，对着太阳擎着它们的叶子，果子，冷静壮丽的神气。它们免不了让那篷帐遮住吗？

免不了。工人们已经扛起他们的杆子，向着
那个地基儿去了。就是那高个儿的还没有走。他
弯下身子去，捻着一小枝的拉芬特草，把他的大
姆指与点人指放在鼻子边，嗅吸了沾着的香气。
老腊看了他那手势，把什么喀拉噶树全忘了，她
就不懂得一个做工人的会注意到那些个东西——
爱拉芬特草的味儿。她认识的能有几个人会做这
样的事。做工人多么异常地有意思呀，她心里
想。为什么她就不能跟做工人的做朋友，强如那
些粗蠢的男孩子们，伴她跳舞的，星期日晚上来
吃夜饭的？他们准是合适得多。

坏处就在，她心里打算，一面那高个的工人
正在一个信封的后背画什么东西，错处就在那些
个可笑的阶级区别，枪毙或是绞死了那一点子就
没有事儿了。就她自个儿说呢，她简直想不着什
么区别不区别。一点儿，一子儿都没有……现在
木槌子打桩的声音已经来了。有人在那儿嘘口
调子，有人唱了出来，"你那儿合适不合适，玛
代？""玛代！"那要好的意思，那——那——她
想表示她多么的快活，让那高个儿的明白她多么

的随便，她多么的瞧不起蠢笨的习惯，老腊就拿起她手里的牛油面包来，狠劲地啃了一大口，一面她瞪着眼看她的小画。她觉得她真是个做工的女孩子似的。

"老腊老腊，你在那儿? 有电话，老腊! "一个声音从屋子里叫了出来。

"来——了! "她就燕子似的掠了去，穿草地，上道儿，上阶沿儿，穿走廊子，进门儿，在前厅里她的爹与老利正在刷他们的帽子，预备办事去。

"我说，老腊，"老利快快地说，"下半天以前你替我看看我的褂子，成不成? 看看要收拾不要。"

"算数。"她说。忽然她自个儿忍不住了。她跑到老利身边。把他小小地，快快地挤了一下。"嘎，我真爱茶会呀，你爱不爱。"老腊喘着气说。

"可——不是。"老利亲密的，孩子的口音说，他也拿他的妹妹挤了一下，把她轻轻地一推。"忙你的电话去，小姐。"

那电话。"对的，对的; 对呀。开弟? 早安，我的乖。来吃中饭？一定来，我的乖。当然好极了。没有东西，就是顶随便的便饭——就是面包壳儿，碎 meringue shells 还有昨天剩下来的什么。是，这早上天气真好不是？等一等——别挂。娘在叫哪。"老腊坐了下来。

"什么，娘？听不着。"

薛太太的声音从楼梯上飘了下来："告诉她还是戴她上礼拜天戴的那顶漂亮帽子。"

"娘说你还是戴你上礼拜天戴的那顶漂亮帽子，好。一点钟，再会。"

老腊放回了听筒，手臂望着脑袋背后一甩，深深地呼了一口气，伸了一个懒腰，手臂又落了下来。"呼，"她叹了口气，快快地重复坐正了。她是静静的，听着。屋子里所有的门户像是全打得大开似的。满屋子只是轻的，快的脚步声，流动的口音。那扇绿布包着的门，通厨房那一带去的，不住地摆着，塞、塞地响。一会儿又听着一个长长的，气呼呼的怪响。那是他们在移动那笨重的钢琴，圆转脚儿擦着地板的声音。但是那空气！要是你静着听，难道那空气总是这样的？小小的，软弱的风在闹着玩儿，一会儿望着窗格子

顶上冲了进来，一会儿带了门儿跑了出去。还有
两小点儿的阳光也在那儿闹着玩儿，一点在墨水
瓶上，一点在白银的照相架上。乖乖的小点子，
尤其是在墨水瓶盖上的那一点。看的顶亲热的。
一个小小的，热热的银星儿。她去亲吻它都成。

前门的小铃子叮的叮的响了，接着沙第印花
布裙子窸窣地上楼梯。一个男子的口音在含糊地
说话，沙第答话，不使劲地，"我不知道呀，等
着，我来问问薛太太。"

"什么事，沙第？"老腊走进了前厅。

"为那卖花的，老腊小姐。"

不错，是的。那边，靠近门儿，一个宽大的
浅盘子，里面满放着一盆盆的粉红百合花儿。就
是一种花。就是百合——"肯那"百合，大的红
的花朵儿，开得满满的，亮亮的，在鲜艳的，深
红色花梗子上长着，简直像有灵性的一样。

"嘎——嘎，沙第！"老腊说，带着小小的哭
声似的。她蹲了下去，像是到百合花的光炎里去
取暖似的；她觉着他们是在她的手指上，在她的
口唇上，在她的心窝里长着。

"错了，"她软音地说，"我们没有定要这么

多的。沙第，去问娘去。”

但是正在这个当儿薛太太也过来了。

“不错的，”她静静地说，“是我定要的。这花儿多么可爱？”她挤紧着老腊的臂膀，“昨天我走过那家花铺子，我在窗子里看着了。我想我这一次总要买他一个痛快。园会不是一个很好的推头吗？”

“可是我以为你说过你不来管我们的事。”老腊说。沙第已经走开了，送花来的小工还靠近他的手车站在门外。她伸出手臂去绕着她娘的项颈，轻轻地，很轻轻地，她咬着他娘的耳朵。

“我的乖孩子，你也不愿意有一个过分刻板的娘不是？别孩子气，挑花的又来了。”

他又拿进了很多的百合花，满满的又是一大盘儿。“一条边地放着，就在进门那儿，门框子的两面，劳驾，”薛太太说，“你看好不好，老腊？”

“好，真好，娘。”

在那客厅里，梅格，玖思，还有那好的小汉士，三个人好容易把那钢琴移好了。

“我说，把这柜子靠着墙，屋子里什么都搬

走，除了椅子，你们看怎么样？"

"成。"

"汉士，把这几个桌子搬到休息室里去，拿一把帚子进来把地毯上的桌腿子痕子扫了——等一等，汉士——"玖思就爱吩咐底下人，他们也爱听她。她那神气就像他们一块儿在唱戏似的。"要太太老腊小姐就上这儿来。"

"就是，玖思小姐。"

她又转身对梅格说话。"我要听听那琴今天成不成，回头下半天他们也许要我唱。我们来试试那 *This Life Is Weary*。"

嘭！他！他，氏！他！那琴声突然很热烈地响了出来，玖思的面色都变了。她握紧了自己的手。她娘同老腊刚进来，她对她们望着。一脸的忧郁，一脸的奥妙。

　　　　这样的生活是疲——倦的，

　　　　一朵眼泪，一声叹气。

　　　　爱情也是要变——心的。

　　　　这样的生活是疲——倦的，

　　　　一朵眼泪，一声叹气。

　　爱情也是不久——长的，

　　时候到了……大家——回去！


　　但是她唱到"大家——回去"的时候，虽则琴声格外地绝望了，她的脸上忽然泛出鲜明的，异常的不同情的笑容。

　　"我的嗓子成不成，妈妈？"她脸上亮着。


　　这样的生活是疲——倦的，

　　希望来了，还是要死的。

　　一场梦景，一场惊醒。


　　但是现在沙第打断了她们。"什么事，沙第？"

　　"说是，太太，厨娘说面包饼上的小纸旗儿有没有？"

　　"面包饼上的小纸旗儿，沙第？"薛太太在梦里似的回响着。那些小孩子一看她的脸就知道她没有小旗儿。

　　"我想想。"一会儿，她对沙第坚定地说，"告诉那厨娘等十分钟我就给她。"

沙第去了。

"我说，老腊，"她母亲快快地说，"跟我到休息间里来。旗子的几个名字我写在一张信封的后背。你来替我写了出来。梅格，马上上楼去，把你头上那湿东西去了。玖思，你也马上去把衣服穿好了。听着了没有，孩子们，要不然回头你们多晚上回家的时候我告诉他，说是——玖思，你要到厨房里去，告那厨娘别着急，好不好？这早上我怕死了她。"

那张信封好容易在饭间里那摆钟背后找了出来。怎么会在那儿，薛太太想都想不着了。

"定是你们里面不知谁从我的手袋里偷了出来，我记得顶清楚的——奶酪几司同柠檬奶冻。写下了没有？"

"写了。"

"鸡子同——"薛太太把那张信封擎得远远的，"什么字，看的像是小老虫。不会是小老虫。不是？"

"青果，宝贝。"老腊说，回过头来望着。

"可不是，青果，对的。这两样东西并着念多怪呀。鸡子同青果。"

她们好容易把那几张旗子写完。老腊就拿走到厨房去了。她见玖思正在那里平厨娘的着急，那厨娘可是一点儿也不怕人。

"我从没有见过这样精巧的面包饼，"玖思乐疯了的口音说，"你说这儿一共有几种，厨娘？十五对不对？"

"十五，玖思小姐。"

"好，厨娘，我恭喜你。"

厨娘手里拿着切面包饼的长刀，抹下了桌上的碎粉屑儿，开了一张嘴尽笑。

"高德铺子里的来了。"沙第喊着，从伙食房里走出来。她看见那人在窗子外面走过。

这就是说奶油松饼来了。高德那家店铺，就是做奶油松饼出名。有了他们的，谁都不愿意自己在家里做。

"去拿进来放在桌子上吧，姑娘。"厨娘吩咐。

沙第去拿了进来，又去了。老腊与玖思当然是长大了，不会认真地见了奶油什么就上劲。可是她们也就忍不住同声地赞美，说这松饼做得真可爱呀。太美了。厨娘动手拾掇，摇下了多余的糖冰。

　　"一见这些个松饼儿，像是你一辈子的茶会全回来了似的，你说是不是?"老腊说。

　　"许有的事，"讲究实际的玖思说，她从不想回到从前去的，"他们看着这样美丽的轻巧，羽毛似的，我说。"

　　"一人拿一个吧，我的乖乖，"厨娘说，她那快乐的口音。"你的妈不会知道的。"

　　这哪儿成。想想，才吃早饭，就吃奶油松饼。一想着都叫人难受。可是要不了两分钟，玖思与老腊都在舐他们的手指儿了，她们那得意的，心里快活的神气，一看就知道她们是才吃了新鲜奶油的。

　　"我们到园里去，从后门出去，"老腊出主意，"我要去看看工人们的篷帐怎么样了。那工人们真有意思。"

　　但是后门的道儿，让厨娘，沙第，高德铺子里的伙计，小汉士几个人拦住了。

　　出了事了。

　　"咯——咯——咯"，厨娘咯咯地叫着，像一只吓慌了的母鸡。沙第的一只手抓紧了她的下

巴，像是牙痛似的。小汉士的脸子像螺旋似的皱
着，摸不清头脑。就是高德铺子里来的伙计看是
自己儿得意似的；这故事是他讲的。

"怎么回事？出了什么事？"

"出了大乱子了，"厨娘说，"一个男子死
了。"

"一个男子死了！哪儿？怎么的？什么时
候？"

但是那店伙计可不愿意现鲜鲜的新闻，让人
家当着他面抢着讲。

"知道那些个小屋子就在这儿下去的，小
姐？"知道？当然她知道。"得，有个年轻的住
在那儿，名字叫司考脱，赶大车儿的。他的马见
了那平道儿的机器，今天早上在霍克路的基角儿
上，他那马见了就发傻，一个斛斗就把他掷了下
去，掷在他脑袋的后背。死了。"

"死了！"老腊瞪着眼望着那伙计。

"他们把他捡起来的时候就死了，"那伙计讲
得更起劲了。"我来的时候正碰着他们把那尸体
抬回家去。"他对着厨娘说，"他剩下一个妻子，
五个小的。"

"玖思，这儿来。"她一把拉住了她妹子的衣袖，牵着她穿过了厨房，到绿布门的那一面。她停下了，靠在门边。"玖思！"她说，吓坏了的，"这怎么办，我们有什么法子把什么事都停了呢？"

"什么事都停了，老腊！"玖思骇然地说，"这怎么讲？"

"把园会停了，当然。"玖思为什么要装假？

但是玖思反而更糊涂了。"把园会停了？老腊我的乖，别那么傻。当然我们不干这样的事。也没有人想我们这么办。别太过分了。"

"可是现鲜鲜地有人死在我们的大门外，我们怎么能举行园会呢？"

这话实在是太过分了，因为那些小屋子有他们自个儿的一条小巷，在她们家一直斜下去的那条街的尽头。中间还隔着一条顶宽的大路哪。不错，他们是太贴近一点。那些小屋子看着真让人眼痛，他们就不应该在这一带的附近。就是几间小小的烂房子，画成朱古律老黄色的。他们的背后园里也就是菜梗子，瘦小的母鸡子，红茄的罐子。他们烟囱里冒出来的烟，先就是寒碜。烂布

似的，烂片似的小烟卷儿，那儿比得上薛家的烟
囱里出来的，那样大片的，银色的羽毛，在天空
里荡着。洗衣服的妇人们住在那条小巷里，还有
扫烟囱的，一个补鞋的，还有一个男的，他的门
前满挂着小雀笼子。孩子们又是成群的。薛家的
孩子小的时候，他们是一步也不准上那儿去的，
怕的是他们学下流话，沾染他们下流的脾气。但
是自从他们长成了，老腊同老利有时也穿着那道
儿走。又肮脏，又讨厌。他们走过都觉得难受。
可是一个人什么地方都得去；什么事情都得亲眼
看。他们就是这样地走过了。

　　"你只要想想我们的音乐队一动手，叫那苦
恼的妇人怎么受得住！"老腊说。

　　"嘎，老腊！"玖思现在认真地着恼了。"要
是每次有人碰着了意外，你的音乐队就得停起
来，你的一辈子也就够受了。我也是比你一样的
难过。我也是一样的软心肠的。"她的眼睛发狠
了。她那盯着她的姊姊的神气，就像是她们小时
候打架的样子。"你这样的感情作用也救不活一
个做工的酒鬼。"她软软地说。

　　"酒鬼！谁说他是酒醉！"老腊也发狠地对着

玖思。"我马上就进去告诉娘去。"她说，正像她从前每次闹翻了说的话。

"请，我的乖。"玖思甜着口音说。

"娘呀，我可以到你的房里吗？"老腊手持着那大的玻璃门拳儿。

"来吧，孩子。唉，怎么回事？怎么的你脸上红红的？"薛太太从她的镜台边转了过来。她正在试她的新帽子。

"娘，有一个人摔死了。"老腊开头说。

"不是在我们的园里？"她娘就打岔。

"不，不！"

"嘎，你真是吓了我一跳。"薛太太叹了口气，放心了，拿下了她的大帽子，放在她的膝腿上。

"可是你听我说，娘。"老腊说。她把这可怕的故事讲了，气都喘不过来。"当然，我们不能开茶会了不是，"她恳求地说，"音乐队，什么人都快到了。他们听得到的，娘；他们差不多是紧邻！"

她娘的态度竟是同玖思方才一样，老腊真骇然了！竟是更难受因为她看是好玩似的。她竟没有把老腊认真。

"但是，我的好孩子，你得应用你的常识。这无非是偶然的，我们听着了那回事。要是那边有人生病了——我就不懂得他们挤在那些脏死的小窠儿里，怎么的活法——我们还不是一样地开我们的茶会不是？"

老腊只好回答说"是的"，可是她心里想这是全错的。她在她娘的沙发椅上坐了下来，捻着那椅垫的绉边。

"娘，这不是我们真的连一点慈悲心都没有了吗？"

"乖孩子！"薛太太站起身走过来了，拿着那帽子。老腊来不及拦阻，她已经把那帽子套在她的头上。"我的孩子！"她娘说，"这帽子是你的。天生是你的。这帽子我戴太嫌年轻，我从没有见过你这样的一张画似的。你自己看看。"她就拿着手镜要她看。

"可是，娘。"老腊又起了一个头。她不能看她自己；她把身子转了过去。

这一来薛太太可也忍不住了，就像方才玖思忍不住了一样。

"你这是太离奇了，老腊，"她冷冷地说，"像他们那样人家也不想我们牺牲什么。况且像你这样要什么人都不乐意，也不见怎样的发善心不是？"

"我不懂。"老腊说，她快快地走了出去，进了她自己的卧房。在那里，很是无意地，她最先见着的，就是镜子里的一个可爱的姑娘，戴着她那黑帽子，金小花儿装边的，还有一条长的黑丝绒带子。她从没有想着过她能有这样的好看。娘是对的吗？她想。现在她竟是希望娘是对的。我不是太过分吗？许是太过分了。就是一转瞬间，她又见着了那可怜的妇人同她的小孩子，她男人的尸体抬到屋子里去。但这都是模糊的，不真切的，像新闻纸上的图画似的。等茶会过了我再想着吧，她定主意了。这像是最妥当的办法了……

中饭吃过一点半。两点半的时候他们已经准备这场闹了。穿绿褂子的音乐队已经到了，在那网球场的基角儿上落座了。

"我的乖！"开第·梅得伦娇音地说，"可不是她们太像青虾蟆？你们应该让他们围着那小池子蹲着，让那领班的站在池中间一张花叶子上。"

老利也到了，一路招呼着进去换衣服了。一见着他，老腊又想起那件祸事了。她要告诉他。如其老利也同其余的见解一样，这就不用说一定是不错的了。她跟着他进了前厅。

"老利！"

"唉！"他已经是半扶梯，但是他转身来见了老腊，他就鼓起了他的腮帮子，睁着大眼睛望着她。"我说，老腊！你叫我眼都看花了，"老利说，"多，多漂亮的帽子！"

老腊轻轻地说："真的吗？"仰着头对老利笑着，到底还是没有告诉他。

不多一会见客人像水一般来了。音乐队动手了，雇来的听差忙着从屋子跑到篷帐里去。随你向哪儿望，总有一对对地在缓缓地走着，弯着身子看花，打招呼，在草地上过去。客人们像是美丽的鸟雀儿，在这下半天停在薛家的园子里，顺路到——哪儿呢？啊，多快活呀，碰着的全是快活人，握着手，贴着脸子，对着眼睛笑。

"老腊乖乖，你多美呀！"

"你的帽子多合适呀，孩子！"

"老腊，你样子顶像西班牙美人，我从没有

见你这样漂亮过。"

老腊抖擞着，也就软软地回答，"你喝了茶没有？来点儿水吧；今天的果子水倒真是别致的。"她跑到她爹那里去，求着他，"好爹爹，音乐队让他们喝点儿水吧？"

这圆满的下午渐渐地成熟了，渐渐地衰谢了，渐渐地花瓣儿全闭着了。

"再没有更满意的园会⋯⋯""大，大成功⋯⋯""真要算是最，最⋯⋯"

老腊帮着她娘说再会。她们一并肩地站在门口，一直等到完事。

"完了，完了，谢谢天，"薛太太说，"把他们全找来，老腊。我们去喝一点新鲜咖啡去。我累坏了。总算是很成功的。可是这些茶会，这些茶会！为什么你们一定不放过要开茶会！"他们全在走空了的篷帐里坐了下来。

"来一块面包夹饼，爹爹。旗子是我写的。"

"多谢。"薛先生咬了一口，那块饼就不见了。他又吃了一块。"我想你们没有听见今天出的骇人的乱子吗？"

"我的乖，"薛太太说，举着她的一只手，"我们听见的。险一点把我们的茶会都弄糟了。老腊硬主张我们把会停了。"

"嘎，娘呀！"老腊不愿意为这件事再受嘲讽。

"总是一件可怕的事情不是？"薛先生说，"那死的也成了家了。就住在这儿下去那个小巷子里，他抛下了一个妻子，半打小孩，他们说。"

很不自然地小静了一会，太太的手弄着她的茶杯，实在爹不识趣了……

忽然她仰起头来望着。桌子上满是那些个面包夹饼，蛋糕，奶油松饼，全没有吃，回头全是没有用的。她想着了她的一个妙主意。

"我知道了，"她说，"我们装起一个篮子来吧。我们拿点儿这完全没有动的上好点心，给那可怜的女人吧。随便怎么样，她的小孩子们总有了一顿大大的食品，你们说对不对？并且她总有邻舍人等出出进进的。不劳她费心这全是现成的，可不是个好主意？"

"老腊！"说着她跳了起来，"把那楼梯边柜子里的那大竹篮子拿来。"

"但是，娘，你难道真以为这是个好主意

吗？"老腊说。

又是一次，多奇怪，她的见解与旁人不同了。拿她们茶会余下的滓子去给人家。那可怜的妇人真的就会乐意吗？

"当然喽！今天你怎么的？方才不多一会儿，你抱怨着人家不发慈悲，可是现在——"

嗳，好的！老腊跑去把篮子拿来了。装满了，堆满了，她娘自己动手的。

"你自己拿了去，乖乖，"她说，"你就是这样去好了。不，等一等，也带一点大红花去。他们那一等人顶喜欢这大花儿的。"

"小心那花梗子毁了她的新花边衣。"讲究实际的玖思说。

真会的。还好，来得及。"那你就拿这竹篮子吧。喂，老腊！"她娘跟她出了篷帐……"随便怎样你可不要……"

"什么，娘？"

不，这种意思还是不装进孩子的脑袋里去好！"没有事！你跑吧！"

老腊关上园门的时候，天已经快黄昏了。一只大狗像一个黑影子似的跑过。这道儿白白地

亮着，望下去那块凹地里暗沉沉的就是那些小
屋子。

过了那半天的热闹这时候多静呀。她现在独
自地走下那斜坡去，到一个地方，那里说是有个
男子死了，她可是有点儿想不清似的。为什么她
想不清？她停步了一会儿。她的内部像满蒙着
亲吻呀，种种的口音呀，杯匙叮当的响声呀，笑
呀，压平的青草味呀，塞得满满的。她再没有余
地，放别的东西。多怪呀！她仰起头望着苍白的
天，她心里想着的就是"对呀，这真是顶满意的
茶会"。

现在那条大路已经走过了。已经近了那小
巷，烟沉沉的黑沉沉的。

披着围巾的女人，戴着粗便帽的男人匆忙地
走着。有的男人靠在木棚子上，小孩子们在门前
玩着。一阵低低的嗡嗡的声响，从那卑污的小屋
子里出来。有的屋子里有一星的灯亮，一个黑影
子，螃蟹似的，在窗子里移动着。老腊低着了头
快快地走。她现在倒抱怨没有裹上一件外衣出
来。她的上身衣闪得多亮呀！还有那黑丝绒飘带
的大帽子——换一顶帽子多好！人家不是望着她

吗？他们一定在望着她。这一来来错了，她早知
道错了。她现在再回去怎么样呢？

　　不，太迟了。这就是那家人家。一定是的，
暗暗的一堆人站在外面。门边一张椅子里坐着一
个很老的老婆子，手里拿着一根拐杖，她在看热
闹，她的一双脚踏在一张报纸上。老腊一走近人
声就停了。这群人也散了。倒像是他们知道她要
到这儿来的似的，像是他们在等着她哪。

　　老腊异常地不自在。颠着她肩上的丝绒带
子，她问一个站在旁边的妇人，"这是司考脱夫
人的家吗？"那个妇人，古怪地笑着，回说："这
是的，小姑娘。"

　　嘎，这情形躲得了多好！她上前他们门前的
走道，伸手敲门的时候，她真的说了，"帮助我，
上帝。"只要躲得了他们那弹出的眼睛，这是有
什么法子把自己裹了起来，裹在一个围肩里都
好。我放下了这篮子就走，她打定了主意。我连
空篮子都不等了。

　　那门开了，一个穿黑的小女人在暗冥里替她
开着门。

　　老腊说，"你是司考脱夫人吗？"但是那女人

的答话吓了老腊一跳，"请进来吧，小姐。"她让她关进在门里了。

"不，"老腊说，"我不进来了，我就要放下这篮子。娘叫我送来——"

在黑沉沉的夹道儿里的小女人像是没有听着似的。"走这儿，请，小姐。"她软媚的口音说，老腊跟了进去。

她进了一间破烂的，又低又窄的厨房，台上一盏冒烟的油灯。灶火的前面有一个妇人坐着。

"哀姆，"引她进去的那个小个儿说，"哀姆，是个小姑娘。"她转身对着老腊。她有意味地说，"我是她的妹子，小姐。您得原谅她不是？"

"嘎，这是当然！"老腊说。"请，请不要打搅她。我——我只要放下——"

但是这时候坐在灶火前的妇人转了过来。她的脸子，肿胀着，红红的，红肿的眼，红肿的口唇，看得可怕。她看是摸不清为什么老腊在那儿。这算什么的意思？为什么一个外客拿着一个篮子站在她的厨房里？这是什么回事？她那可怜的脸子又是紧紧地皱了起来。

"我有数，"还有那个说，"我会谢小姑娘

的。"

她又说了，"您得原谅她，小姐，我想你一
定。"她的脸子，也是肿肿的，想来一个讨好的
笑容。

老腊只求马上出得去，马上走开，她已经回
上了那条板弄。那门开了，她一直走过去，走进
那间卧房，那死人就摊在那里。

"您得看看他不是？"哀姆的妹子说，她匆匆
地跑上前去到那床边，"不要怕，我的姑娘，"——
现在她的口音变了很爱惜，很机敏似的，她爱怜
地把死人身上的被单拉下了，——"他像一幅画。
什么怪相也没有。过来，我的乖。"

老腊过来了。

一个年轻的人躺在那里，深深地睡着——
睡这样地着，这样地深，他看是离他们俩远着
哪。嘎，这样隔着远远的，这样地平静。他在做
梦，从此不要惊醒他了。他的头深深地落在枕头
上，他的眼紧闭着，眼睛在紧闭了的眼睛里是盲
的了。他全交给他的梦了。什么园会呀，竹篮子
呀，花边衣呀，与他有什么相干。他离开那些个
事情远着哪。他是神奇的，美丽的了。一面他们

在那里欢笑，一面音乐队在那里奏乐，这件不可思议的事到了这条小巷里。快活……快活……什么都好了，睡着的脸子在说。这正是该的，我是满足了。

但是我总得哭一哭，她要出这屋子总得对他说几句话。老腊响响地孩子似的哭了一声。

"饶恕我的帽子。"她说。

这时候她也不等哀姆的妹子了。她自己走出了门，下了走道，经过那些黑沉沉的人们。在那巷子的转角上她碰着了老利。

他从黑荫里走了出来。"是你吗，老腊？"

"是我。"

"娘着急了，没有什么吗？"

"是，很好。嘎，老利！"她挽住他的臂膀，紧紧地靠着他。

"我说，你没有哭不是？"她的兄弟问。

老腊摇着她的头，她是哭着哩。

老利拿手围着她的肩膀。"不要哭，"他那亲热的，爱怜的口音说，"那边难受不是？"

"不，"老腊悲哽地说，"这太不可思议了，但是，老利——"她停顿了，她望着她的兄弟。

"生命是不是，"她打顿地说，"生命是不是——"
但是生命是什么她说不上，不碍，他很懂得。"可
不是，乖乖? "老利说。


　　　　　十月二十九日下午二时译完

# *The Garden Party*

*A*nd after all the weather was ideal. They could not have had a more perfect day for a garden-party if they had ordered it. Windless, warm, the sky without a cloud. Only the blue was veiled with a haze of light gold, as it is sometimes in early summer. The gardener had been up since dawn, mowing the lawns and sweeping them, until the grass and the dark flat rosettes where the daisy plants had been seemed to shine. As for the roses, you could not help feeling they understood that roses are the only flowers that impress people at garden-parties; the only flowers that everybody is certain of knowing. Hundreds, yes, literally hundreds, had come out in a single night; the green bushes bowed down as though they had been visited by archangels.

Breakfast was not yet over before the men came

to put up the marquee.

"Where do you want the marquee put, mother?"

"My dear child, it's no use asking me. I'm determined to leave everything to you children this year. Forget I am your mother. Treat me as an honoured guest."

But Meg could not possibly go and supervise the men. She had washed her hair before breakfast, and she sat drinking her coffee in a green turban, with a dark wet curl stamped on each cheek. Jose, the butterfly, always came down in a silk petticoat and a kimono jacket.

"You'll have to go, Laura; you're the artistic one."

Away Laura flew, still holding her piece of bread-and-butter. It's so delicious to have an excuse for eating out of doors, and besides, she loved having to arrange things; she always felt she could do it so much better than anybody else.

Four men in their shirt-sleeves stood grouped together on the garden path. They carried staves covered with rolls of canvas, and they had big tool-bags slung on their backs. They looked impressive. Laura wished now that she had not got the bread-and-butter, but there was nowhere to put it, and she couldn't possibly throw it away. She blushed and tried to look severe and even a little bit short-sighted as she came up to them.

"Good morning," she said, copying her mother's voice. But that sounded so fearfully affected that she was ashamed, and stammered like a little girl, "Oh—er—have you come—is it about the marquee?"

"That's right, miss," said the tallest of the men, a lanky, freckled fellow, and he shifted his tool-bag, knocked back his straw hat and smiled down at her. "That's about it."

His smile was so easy, so friendly that Laura recovered. What nice eyes he had, small, but such a dark blue! And now she looked at the others, they were smiling too. "Cheer up, we won't bite," their smile seemed to say. How very nice workmen were! And what a beautiful morning! She mustn't mention the morning; she must be business-like. The marquee.

"Well, what about the lily-lawn? Would that do?"

And she pointed to the lily-lawn with the hand that didn't hold the bread-and-butter. They turned, they stared in the direction. A little fat chap thrust out his under-lip, and the tall fellow frowned.

"I don't fancy it," said he. "Not conspicuous enough. You see, with a thing like a marquee," and he turned to Laura in his easy way, "you want to put it somewhere where it'll give you a bang slap in the eye, if you follow me."

Laura's upbringing made her wonder for a moment whether it was quite respectful of a workman to talk to her of bangs slap in the eye. But she did quite follow him.

"A corner of the tennis-court," she suggested. "But the band's going to be in one corner."

"H'm, going to have a band, are you?" said another of the workmen. He was pale. He had a haggard look as his dark eyes scanned the tennis-court. What was he thinking?

"Only a very small band," said Laura gently. Perhaps he wouldn't mind so much if the band was quite small. But the tall fellow interrupted.

"Look here, miss, that's the place. Against those trees. Over there. That'll do fine."

Against the karakas. Then the karaka-trees would be hidden. And they were so lovely, with their broad, gleaming leaves, and their clusters of yellow fruit. They were like trees you imagined growing on a desert island, proud, solitary, lifting their leaves and fruits to the sun in a kind of silent splendour. Must they be hidden by a marquee?

They must. Already the men had shouldered their staves and were making for the place. Only the tall fellow was left. He bent down, pinched a sprig of lavender, put his thumb and forefinger to his nose and snuffed up the smell. When Laura saw that gesture she forgot all about the karakas in her wonder at him caring for things like that—caring for the smell of lavender. How many men that she knew would have done such a thing? Oh, how extraordinarily nice workmen were, she thought. Why couldn't she have workmen for her friends rather than the silly boys she danced with and who came to Sunday night supper? She would get on much better with men like these.

It's all the fault, she decided, as the tall fellow drew something on the back of an envelope, something that was to be looped up or left to hang, of these absurd class distinctions. Well, for her part, she didn't feel them. Not a bit, not an atom... And now there came the chock-chock of wooden hammers. Some one whistled, some one sang out, "Are you right there, matey?" "Matey!" The friendliness of it, the—the—Just to prove how happy she was, just to show the tall fellow how at home she felt, and how she despised stupid conventions, Laura took a big bite of her bread-and-butter as she stared at the little drawing. She felt just like a work-girl.

"Laura, Laura, where are you? Telephone, Laura!" a voice cried from the house.

"Coming!" Away she skimmed, over the lawn,

up the path, up the steps, across the veranda, and into the porch. In the hall her father and Laurie were brushing their hats ready to go to the office.

"I say, Laura," said Laurie very fast, "you might just give a squiz at my coat before this afternoon. See if it wants pressing."

"I will," said she. Suddenly she couldn't stop herself. She ran at Laurie and gave him a small, quick squeeze. "Oh, I do love parties, don't you?" gasped Laura.

"Ra-ther," said Laurie's warm, boyish voice, and he squeezed his sister too, and gave her a gentle push. "Dash off to the telephone, old girl."

The telephone. "Yes, yes; oh yes. Kitty? Good morning, dear. Come to lunch? Do, dear. Delighted of course. It will only be a very scratch meal—just the sandwich crusts and broken meringue-shells and what's left over. Yes, isn't it a perfect morning? Your white? Oh, I certainly should. One moment— hold the line. Mother's calling." And Laura sat back. "What, mother? Can't hear."

Mrs. Sheridan's voice floated down the stairs. "Tell her to wear that sweet hat she had on last Sunday."

"Mother says you're to wear that sweet hat you had on last Sunday. Good. One o'clock. Bye-bye."

Laura put back the receiver, flung her arms over her head, took a deep breath, stretched and let them fall. "Huh," she sighed, and the moment after the sigh she sat up quickly. She was still, listening. All the doors in the house seemed to be open. The house was alive with soft, quick steps and running voices. The green baize door that led to the kitchen regions swung open and shut with a muffled thud. And now there came a long, chuckling absurd sound. It was the heavy piano being moved on its stiff castors. But the air! If you stopped to notice, was the air always like this? Little faint winds were playing chase, in at the tops of the windows, out at the doors. And there were two tiny spots of sun, one on the inkpot, one on a silver photograph frame, playing too. Darling little spots. Especially the one on the inkpot lid. It was quite warm. A warm little silver star. She could have kissed it.

The front door bell pealed, and there sounded the rustle of Sadie's print skirt on the stairs. A man's voice murmured; Sadie answered, careless, "I'm sure I don't know. Wait. I'll ask Mrs. Sheridan."

"What is it, Sadie?" Laura came into the hall.

"It's the florist, Miss. Laura."

It was, indeed. There, just inside the door, stood a wide, shallow tray full of pots of pink lilies. No other kind. Nothing but lilies—canna lilies, big pink flowers, wide open, radiant, almost frighteningly alive on bright crimson stems.

"O-oh, Sadie!" said Laura, and the sound was like a little moan. She crouched down as if to warm herself at that blaze of lilies; she felt they were in her fingers, on her lips, growing in her breast.

"It's some mistake," she said faintly. "Nobody ever ordered so many. Sadie, go and find mother."

But at that moment Mrs. Sheridan joined them.

"It's quite right," she said calmly. "Yes, I ordered them. Aren't they lovely?" She pressed Laura's arm.

"I was passing the shop yesterday, and I saw them in the window. And I suddenly thought for once in my life I shall have enough canna lilies. The garden-party will be a good excuse."

"But I thought you said you didn't mean to interfere," said Laura. Sadie had gone. The florist's man was still outside at his van. She put her arm round her mother's neck and gently, very gently, she bit her mother's ear.

"My darling child, you wouldn't like a logical mother, would you? Don't do that. Here's the man."

He carried more lilies still, another whole tray.

"Bank them up, just inside the door, on both sides of the porch, please," said Mrs. Sheridan. "Don't you agree, Laura?"

"Oh, I do, mother."

In the drawing-room Meg, Jose and good little Hans had at last succeeded in moving the piano.

"Now, if we put this chesterfield against the wall and move everything out of the room except the chairs, don't you think?"

"Quite."

"Hans, move these tables into the smoking-room, and bring a sweeper to take these marks off the carpet and—one moment, Hans—" Jose loved giving orders to the servants, and they loved obeying her. She always made them feel they were taking part in some drama. "Tell mother and Miss Laura to come here at once."

"Very good, Miss Jose."

She turned to Meg. "I want to hear what the piano sounds like, just in case I'm asked to sing this afternoon. Let's try over 'This life is Weary'."

Pom! Ta-ta-ta Tee-ta! The piano burst out so passionately that Jose's face changed. She clasped her hands. She looked mournfully and enigmatically at her mother and Laura as they came in.

> *This Life is Wee-ary,*
> *A Tear—a Sigh.*
> *A Love that Chan-ges,*
> *This Life is Wee-ary,*

*A Tear—a Sigh.*

*A Love that Chan-ges,*

*And then... Good-bye!*


But at the word "Good-bye", and although the piano sounded more desperate than ever, her face broke into a brilliant, dreadfully unsympathetic smile.

"Aren't I in good voice, mummy?" she beamed.


*This Life is Wee-ary,*

*Hope comes to Die.*

*A Dream—a Wa-kening.*


But now Sadie interrupted them. "What is it, Sadie?"

"If you please, m'm, cook says have you got the flags for the sandwiches?"

"The flags for the sandwiches, Sadie?" echoed Mrs. Sheridan dreamily. And the children knew by her face that she hadn't got them. "Let me see." And she said to Sadie firmly, "Tell cook I'll let her have them in ten minutes."

Sadie went.

"Now, Laura," said her mother quickly, "come with me into the smoking-room. I've got the names somewhere on the back of an envelope. You'll have to write them out for me. Meg, go upstairs this minute and take that wet thing off your head. Jose, run and finish dressing this instant. Do you hear me, children, or shall I have to tell your father when he comes home to-night? And—and, Jose, pacify cook if you do go into the kitchen, will you? I'm terrified of her this morning."

The envelope was found at last behind the dining-room clock, though how it had got there Mrs. Sheridan could not imagine.

"One of you children must have stolen it out of my bag, because I remember vividly—cream cheese and lemon-curd. Have you done that?"

"Yes."

"Egg and—" Mrs. Sheridan held the envelope

away from her. "It looks like mice. It can't be mice, can it?"

"Olive, pet," said Laura, looking over her shoulder.

"Yes, of course, olive. What a horrible combination it sounds. Egg and olive."

They were finished at last, and Laura took them off to the kitchen. She found Jose there pacifying the cook, who did not look at all terrifying.

"I have never seen such exquisite sandwiches," said Jose's rapturous voice. "How many kinds did you say there were, cook? Fifteen?"

"Fifteen, Miss Jose."

"Well, cook, I congratulate you."

Cook swept up crusts with the long sandwich knife, and smiled broadly.

"Godber's has come," announced Sadie, issuing out of the pantry. She had seen the man pass the window.

That meant the cream puffs had come. Godber's were famous for their cream puffs. Nobody ever thought of making them at home.

"Bring them in and put them on the table, my girl," ordered cook.

Sadie brought them in and went back to the door. Of course Laura and Jose were far too grown-up to really care about such things. All the same, they couldn't help agreeing that the puffs looked very attractive. Very. Cook began arranging them, shaking off the extra icing sugar.

"Don't they carry one back to all one's parties?" said Laura.

"I suppose they do," said practical Jose, who never liked to be carried back. "They look beautifully light and feathery, I must say."

"Have one each, my dears," said cook in her comfortable voice. "Yer ma won't know."

Oh, impossible. Fancy cream puffs so soon after breakfast. The very idea made one shudder. All the same, two minutes later Jose and Laura were licking their fingers with that absorbed inward look that only comes from whipped cream.

"Let's go into the garden, out by the back way," suggested Laura. "I want to see how the men are getting on with the marquee. They're such awfully nice men."

But the back door was blocked by cook, Sadie, Godber's man and Hans.

Something had happened.

"Tuk-tuk-tuk," clucked cook like an agitated hen. Sadie had her hand clapped to her cheek as though she had toothache. Hans's face was screwed up in the effort to understand. Only Godber's man seemed to be enjoying himself; it was his story.

"What's the matter? What's happened?"

"There's been a horrible accident," said Cook. "A man killed."

"A man killed! Where? How? When?"

But Godber's man wasn't going to have his story snatched from under his very nose.

"Know those little cottages just below here, miss?" Know them? Of course, she knew them. "Well, there's a young chap living there, name of

Scott, a carter. His horse shied at a traction-engine, corner of Hawke Street this morning, and he was thrown out on the back of his head. Killed."

"Dead!" Laura stared at Godber's man.

"Dead when they picked him up," said Godber's man with relish. "They were taking the body home as I come up here." And he said to the cook, "He's left a wife and five little ones."

"Jose, come here." Laura caught hold of her sister's sleeve and dragged her through the kitchen to the other side of the green baize door. There she paused and leaned against it. "Jose!" she said, horrified, "however are we going to stop everything?"

"Stop everything, Laura!" cried Jose in astonishment. "What do you mean?"

"Stop the garden-party, of course." Why did Jose pretend?

But Jose was still more amazed. "Stop the garden-party? My dear Laura, don't be so absurd. Of course we can't do anything of the kind. Nobody expects us to. Don't be so extravagant."

"But we can't possibly have a garden-party with a
man dead just outside the front gate."

That really was extravagant, for the little cottages
were in a lane to themselves at the very bottom of a
steep rise that led up to the house. A broad road ran
between. True, they were far too near. They were
the greatest possible eyesore, and they had no right
to be in that neighbourhood at all. They were little
mean dwellings painted a chocolate brown. In the
garden patches there was nothing but cabbage stalks,
sick hens and tomato cans. The very smoke coming
out of their chimneys was poverty-stricken. Little
rags and shreds of smoke, so unlike the great silvery
plumes that uncurled from the Sheridans' chimneys.
Washerwomen lived in the lane and sweeps and a
cobbler, and a man whose house-front was studded
all over with minute bird-cages. Children swarmed.
When the Sheridans were little they were forbidden
to set foot there because of the revolting language
and of what they might catch. But since they

were grown up, Laura and Laurie on their prowls sometimes walked through. It was disgusting and sordid. They came out with a shudder. But still one must go everywhere; one must see everything. So through they went.

"And just think of what the band would sound like to that poor woman," said Laura.

"Oh, Laura!" Jose began to be seriously annoyed. "If you're going to stop a band playing every time some one has an accident, you'll lead a very strenuous life. I'm every bit as sorry about it as you. I feel just as sympathetic." Her eyes hardened. She looked at her sister just as she used to when they were little and fighting together. "You won't bring a drunken workman back to life by being sentimental," she said softly.

"Drunk! Who said he was drunk?" Laura turned furiously on Jose. She said, just as they had used to say on those occasions, "I'm going straight up to tell mother."

"Do, dear," cooed Jose.

"Mother, can I come into your room?" Laura turned the big glass door-knob.

"Of course, child. Why, what's the matter? What's given you such a colour?" And Mrs. Sheridan turned round from her dressing-table. She was trying on a new hat.

"Mother, a man's been killed," began Laura.

"Not in the garden?" interrupted her mother.

"No, no!"

"Oh, what a fright you gave me!" Mrs. Sheridan sighed with relief, and took off the big hat and held it on her knees.

"But listen, mother," said Laura. Breathless, half-choking, she told the dreadful story. "Of course, we can't have our party, can we?" she pleaded. "The band and everybody arriving. They'd hear us, mother; they're nearly neighbours!"

To Laura's astonishment her mother behaved just like Jose; it was harder to bear because she seemed amused. She refused to take Laura seriously.

"But, my dear child, use your common sense. It's

only by accident we've heard of it. If some one had died there normally—and I can't understand how they keep alive in those poky little holes—we should still be having our party, shouldn't we?"

Laura had to say "yes" to that, but she felt it was all wrong. She sat down on her mother's sofa and pinched the cushion frill.

"Mother, isn't it terribly heartless of us?" she asked.

"Darling!" Mrs. Sheridan got up and came over to her, carrying the hat. Before Laura could stop her she had popped it on. "My child!" said her mother, "the hat is yours. It's made for you. It's much too young for me. I have never seen you look such a picture. Look at yourself!" And she held up her hand-mirror.

"But, mother," Laura began again. She couldn't look at herself; she turned aside.

This time Mrs. Sheridan lost patience just as Jose had done.

"You are being very absurd, Laura," she said coldly. "People like that don't expect sacrifices from us. And it's not very sympathetic to spoil everybody's enjoyment as you're doing now."

"I don't understand," said Laura, and she walked quickly out of the room into her own bedroom. There, quite by chance, the first thing she saw was this charming girl in the mirror, in her black hat trimmed with gold daisies, and a long black velvet ribbon. Never had she imagined she could look like that. Is mother right? she thought. And now she hoped her mother was right. Am I being extravagant? Perhaps it was extravagant. Just for a moment she had another glimpse of that poor woman and those little children, and the body being carried into the house. But it all seemed blurred, unreal, like a picture in the newspaper. I'll remember it again after the party's over, she decided. And somehow that seemed quite the best plan...

Lunch was over by half-past one. By half-past two they were all ready for the fray. The green-coated band had arrived and was established in a corner of the tennis-court.

"My dear!" trilled Kitty Maitland, "aren't they too like frogs for words? You ought to have arranged them round the pond with the conductor in the middle on a leaf."

Laurie arrived and hailed them on his way to dress. At the sight of him Laura remembered the accident again. She wanted to tell him. If Laurie agreed with the others, then it was bound to be all right. And she followed him into the hall.

"Laurie!"

"Hallo!" He was half-way upstairs, but when he turned round and saw Laura he suddenly puffed out his cheeks and goggled his eyes at her. "My word, Laura! You do look stunning," said Laurie. "What an absolutely topping hat!"

Laura said faintly "Is it?" and smiled up at Laurie, and didn't tell him after all.

Soon after that people began coming in streams. The band struck up; the hired waiters ran from the house to the marquee. Wherever you looked there were couples strolling, bending to the flowers, greeting, moving on over the lawn. They were like bright birds that had alighted in the Sheridans' garden for this one afternoon, on their way to—where? Ah, what happiness it is to be with people who all are happy, to press hands, press cheeks, smile into eyes.

"Darling Laura, how well you look!"

"What a becoming hat, child!"

"Laura, you look quite Spanish. I've never seen you look so striking."

And Laura, glowing, answered softly, "Have you had tea? Won't you have an ice? The passion-fruit ices really are rather special." She ran to her father and begged him. "Daddy darling, can't the band have something to drink?"

And the perfect afternoon slowly ripened, slowly faded, slowly its petals closed.

"Never a more delightful garden-party... " "The greatest success... " "Quite the most... "

Laura helped her mother with the good-byes. They stood side by side in the porch till it was all over.

"All over, all over, thank heaven," said Mrs. Sheridan. "Round up the others, Laura. Let's go and have some fresh coffee. I'm exhausted. Yes, it's been very successful. But oh, these parties, these parties! Why will you children insist on giving parties!" And they all of them sat down in the deserted marquee.

"Have a sandwich, daddy dear. I wrote the flag."

"Thanks." Mr. Sheridan took a bite and the sandwich was gone. He took another. "I suppose you didn't hear of a beastly accident that happened to-day?" he said.

"My dear," said Mrs. Sheridan, holding up her hand, "we did. It nearly ruined the party. Laura insisted we should put it off."

"Oh, mother!" Laura didn't want to be teased about it.

"It was a horrible affair all the same," said Mr. Sheridan. "The chap was married too. Lived just below in the lane, and leaves a wife and half a dozen kiddies, so they say."

An awkward little silence fell. Mrs. Sheridan fidgeted with her cup. Really, it was very tactless of father...

Suddenly she looked up. There on the table were all those sandwiches, cakes, puffs, all uneaten, all going to be wasted. She had one of her brilliant ideas.

"I know," she said. "Let's make up a basket. Let's send that poor creature some of this perfectly good food. At any rate, it will be the greatest treat for the children. Don't you agree? And she's sure to have neighbours calling in and so on. What a point to have it all ready prepared. Laura!" She jumped up. "Get me the big basket out of the stairs cupboard."

"But, mother, do you really think it's a good idea?" said Laura.

Again, how curious, she seemed to be different from them all. To take scraps from their party. Would the poor woman really like that?

"Of course! What's the matter with you to-day? An hour or two ago you were insisting on us being sympathetic, and now—"

Oh well! Laura ran for the basket. It was filled, it was heaped by her mother.

"Take it yourself, darling," said she. "Run down just as you are. No, wait, take the arum lilies too. People of that class are so impressed by arum lilies."

"The stems will ruin her lace frock," said practical Jose.

So they would. Just in time. "Only the basket, then. And, Laura!"—her mother followed her out of the marquee— "don't on any account—"

"What mother?"

No, better not put such ideas into the child's head! "Nothing! Run along."

It was just growing dusky as Laura shut their garden gates. A big dog ran by like a shadow. The road gleamed white, and down below in the hollow the little cottages were in deep shade. How quiet it seemed after the afternoon. Here she was going down the hill to somewhere where a man lay dead, and she couldn't realize it. Why couldn't she? She stopped a minute. And it seemed to her that kisses, voices, tinkling spoons, laughter, the smell of crushed grass were somehow inside her. She had no room for anything else. How strange! She looked up at the pale sky, and all she thought was, "Yes, it was the most successful party."

Now the broad road was crossed. The lane began, smoky and dark. Women in shawls and men's tweed caps hurried by. Men hung over the palings; the children played in the doorways. A low hum came from the mean little cottages. In some of them there was a flicker of light, and a shadow, crab-like, moved across the window. Laura bent her head and hurried on. She wished now she had put on a coat. How her frock shone! And the big hat with the velvet streamer—if only it was another hat! Were the people looking at her? They must be. It was a mistake to have come; she knew all along it was a mistake. Should she go back even now?

No, too late. This was the house. It must be. A dark knot of people stood outside. Beside the gate an old, old woman with a crutch sat in a chair, watching. She had her feet on a newspaper. The voices stopped as Laura drew near. The group parted. It was as though she was expected, as though they had known she was coming here.

Laura was terribly nervous. Tossing the velvet ribbon over her shoulder, she said to a woman standing by, "Is this Mrs. Scott's house?" and the woman, smiling queerly, said, "It is, my lass."

Oh, to be away from this! She actually said, "Help me, God," as she walked up the tiny path and knocked. To be away from those staring eyes, or to be covered up in anything, one of those women's shawls even. I'll just leave the basket and go, she decided. I shan't even wait for it to be emptied.

Then the door opened. A little woman in black showed in the gloom.

Laura said, "Are you Mrs. Scott?" But to her horror the woman answered, "Walk in please, miss," and she was shut in the passage.

"No," said Laura, "I don't want to come in. I only

want to leave this basket. Mother sent—"

The little woman in the gloomy passage seemed not to have heard her. "Step this way, please, miss," she said in an oily voice, and Laura followed her.

She found herself in a wretched little low kitchen, lighted by a smoky lamp. There was a woman sitting before the fire.

"Em," said the little creature who had let her in. "Em! It's a young lady." She turned to Laura. She said meaningly, "I'm 'er sister, miss. You'll excuse 'er, won't you?"

"Oh, but of course!" said Laura. "Please, please don't disturb her. I—I only want to leave—"

But at that moment the woman at the fire turned round. Her face, puffed up, red, with swollen eyes and swollen lips, looked terrible. She seemed as though she couldn't understand why Laura was there. What did it mean? Why was this stranger standing in the kitchen with a basket? What was it all about? And the poor face puckered up again.

"All right, my dear," said the other. "I'll thank the

young lady."

And again she began, "You'll excuse her, miss, I'm sure," and her face, swollen too, tried an oily smile.

Laura only wanted to get out, to get away. She was back in the passage. The door opened. She walked straight through into the bedroom, where the dead man was lying.

"You'd like a look at 'im, wouldn't you?" said Em's sister, and she brushed past Laura over to the bed. "Don't be afraid, my lass,"—and now her voice sounded fond and sly, and fondly she drew down the sheet—" "'e looks a picture. There's nothing to show. Come along, my dear."

Laura came.

There lay a young man, fast asleep—sleeping so soundly, so deeply, that he was far, far away from them both. Oh, so remote, so peaceful. He was dreaming. Never wake him up again. His head was sunk in the pillow, his eyes were closed; they were blind under the closed eyelids. He was given up to his dream. What did garden-parties and baskets and lace frocks matter to him? He was far from all those things. He was wonderful, beautiful. While they were laughing and while the band was playing, this marvel had come to the lane. Happy... happy... All is well, said that sleeping face. This is just as it should be. I am content.

But all the same you had to cry, and she couldn't go out of the room without saying something to him. Laura gave a loud childish sob.

"Forgive my hat," she said.

And this time she didn't wait for Em's sister. She found her way out of the door, down the path, past all those dark people. At the corner of the lane she met Laurie.

He stepped out of the shadow. "Is that you, Laura?"

"Yes."

"Mother was getting anxious. Was it all right?"

"Yes, quite. Oh, Laurie!" She took his arm, she pressed up against him.

"I say, you're not crying, are you?" asked her

brother.

Laura shook her head. She was.

Laurie put his arm round her shoulder. "Don't cry," he said in his warm, loving voice. "Was it awful?"

"No," sobbed Laura. "It was simply marvellous. But Laurie—" She stopped, she looked at her brother. "Isn't life," she stammered, "isn't life—" But what life was she couldn't explain. No matter. He quite understood.

"Isn't it, darling?" said Laurie.

# 一 杯 茶

　　费蔷媚并不怎样地美。不，你不会得叫她美。好看？哦是的，要是你把她分开来看……可是为什么要拿一个好好的人分开来看，这不太惨了吗？她年纪是轻的，够漂亮，十分地时新，穿衣服讲究极了的，专念最新出的新书博学极了的，上她家去的是一群趣极了的杂凑，社会上顶重要的人物以及……美术家——怪东西，她自己的"发现"，有几个怕得死人的，可也有看得过好玩的。

　　蔷媚结婚二年了。她有一个蜜甜的孩子，男的。不，不是彼得——叫密仡儿。她的丈夫简直是爱透了她的。他们家有钱，真的有钱，不是就只够舒服过去一类，那听着寒碜，闷劲儿的，像是提起谁家的祖老太爷祖老太太。他们可不，蔷媚要什么东西，她就到巴黎去买，不比你我就知道到彭德街去。她要买花的话，她那车就在黎锦街上那家上等花铺子门前停住了，蔷媚走进铺子去扁着她那眼，带"洋味儿"的看法，口里说："我要那些那些。那个给我四把。那一瓶子的玫瑰全要。哦，那瓶子也让我带了去吧。不，不要丁香。我恨丁香。那花不是样儿。"铺子里的伙计弯着身子，拿丁香另放在一个看不见的地方，倒像她那话正说对了似的，丁香是真不是样儿。"给我那一球矮个儿的黄水仙。那红的白的也拿着。"她走出铺子上车去的时候，就有一个瘦小的女孩子一颠一颠地跟在背后，抱着一个多大的白纸包的花，像是一个孩子裹在长抱裙里似的……

一个冬天的下午她在寇崇街上一家古董铺里买东西。她喜欢那铺子。他那儿先就清静，不提别的，你去往往可以独占，再兼那铺子里的掌柜，也不知怎么的，就爱伺候她。她一进门儿，他不提有多快活。他抱紧了他自个儿的手；他感激得话都说不出来。恭维，当然。可还是的，这铺子有意思……

"你明白，太太，"他总是用他那恭敬的低音调讲话，"我宝贵我的东西。我宁可留着不卖的，与其卖给不识货的主顾，他们没有那细心，最难得的……"

一边深深地呼着气，他手里拿一小方块的蓝丝绒给展开了，放在玻璃柜上，用他那没血色的指尖儿按着。

今天的是一只小盒子。他替她留着的。他谁都没有给看过的。一只精致的小珐琅盒儿，那釉光真不错，看得就像是在奶酪里焙成的。那盖上雕盖一个小人儿站在一株开花的树底下，还有一个更小的小人儿还伸着她那一双手搂着他哪。她的帽子，就够小绣球花的花瓣儿大，挂在一个树枝上；还有绿的飘带。半天里还有一朵粉红的云彩在他们的头顶浮着，像一个探消息的天使。蔷媚把她自己的手从她那长手套里探了出来。她每回看这类东西总是褪了手套的。哦，她很喜欢这个。她爱它，它是个小宝贝。她一定得留了它。她拿那奶光的盒儿反复地看，打开了又给关上，她不由地注意到她自个儿的一双手，衬着柜上那块蓝丝绒，不提够多好看。那掌柜的，在他心里那一个不透亮的地基儿，也许竟敢容留同样的感想。因为他手拿着一管铅笔，身子靠在玻璃柜上，他那白得没血色的手指儿心虚虚地向着她那玫瑰色发艳光地爬着，一边他喃喃地说着话："太太你要是许我点给你看，那小人儿的上身衣上还刻着花哪。"

"有意思！"蔷媚喜欢那些花。这要多少钱呢？有一晌掌柜的像是没有听见。这回她听得他低声地说了，"二十八个金几尼，太太。"

"二十八个几尼。"蔷媚没有给回音。她放下了那小盒儿；她扣上了她的手套。二十八个几尼。就有钱也不能……她愣着了。她一眼瞟着了一把肥肥的水壶，像一只肥肥的母鸡蹲在那掌柜的头上似的，她答话的口音还有点儿迷糊的："好吧，替我留着——行不行？我想……"

但是那掌柜的已经鞠过躬，表示遵命，意思仿佛是替她留着是他唯一的使命。他愿意，当然，永远替她留着。

那扇谨慎的门咄地关上了。她站在门外的台阶上，看着这冬天的下午。正下着雨，下雨天就跟着昏，黑夜的影子像灰沙似的在半空里洒下来。空气里有一股冷的涩的味儿，新亮上的街灯看着凄惨。对街屋子里的灯光也是这阴瑟瑟的。

它们暗暗地亮着像是惆怅什么。街上人匆匆地来往，全躲在他们可恨的伞子底下。蔷媚觉着一阵子古怪的心沉。她拿手筒窝紧了她的胸口；她心想要有那小盒子一起窝着多好。那车当然在那儿。边街就是的，可是她还待着不动。做人有时候的情景真叫你惊心，就这从屋子里探身出来看着外边的世界，哪儿都是愁，够多难受。你可不能因此就让打失了兴致，你应当跑回家去，吃他一顿特别预备的茶点。但她正想到这儿的时候，一个年轻的女孩子，瘦的，黑的，鬼影子似的——她哪儿来的？——贴近蔷媚的肘子旁边站着，一个小声音，像是叹气，又像是哭，在说着话："太太，你许我跟你说一句话吧？"

"跟我说话？"蔷媚转过身子去。她见一个小个儿的破烂的女子睁着一双大眼珠，年纪倒是轻的，不比她自己大，一双冻红的手抓着她的领口，浑身发着抖，像是才从凉水里爬起来似的。

"太——太太，"那声音发愣地叫着，"你能不能给我够吃一杯茶的钱？"

"一杯茶？"听那声音倒是直白老实的；一点也不像花子的口气。"那你一个子儿也没有吗？"

蔷媚问。

"没有，太太。"她回答。

"多奇怪！"蔷媚冲着黄昏的微光直瞧，那女子的眼光也向她瞪着。这不比奇怪还奇怪！蔷媚忽然间觉到这倒是个奇遇。竟像是陀思妥耶夫斯基小说里出来的，这黑夜间的相逢。她就带这女子回家去又怎么呢？她就试演演她常常在小说里戏台上看到的一类事情，看他下文怎么来，好不好呢？这准够耸荡的。她仿佛听着她自己事后对她的朋友们说："我简直地就带了她回家。"这时候她走上一步，对她身旁暗沉沉的人影儿说："跟我回家吃茶去。"

那女子吓得往后退。她给吓得连哆嗦都停了一阵子。蔷媚伸出一只手去，按着她的臂膀。"我不诳你。"她说，微微地笑着。她觉得她的笑够直爽够和气的。"来吧，为什么不？坐了我车一共回家吃茶去。"

"你——你不能是这个意思，太太。"那女子说，她的声音里有苦痛。

"是的哪，"蔷媚叫着，"我是要你去。你去我欢喜，来你的。"

　　那女子拿她的手指盖住她的口,眼睁得老大地盯着蔷媚。"你——你不是带我到警察局去?"她愣着说。

　　"警察局!"蔷媚发笑了。"我为什么要那么恶?不,我就要你去暖和暖和,乘便听听——你愿意告诉我的话。"

　　饿慌了的人是容易被带走的。小车夫拉开了车门,不一忽儿她们在昏沉的街道上飞似的去了。

　　"得!"蔷媚说。她觉着得胜了似的,她的手溜进了套手的丝绒带。她眼看着她钩住的小俘虏,心里直想说,"这我可逮住你了。"她当然是好意。喔,岂但好意。她意思要做给这女子看,叫她相信——这世界上有的是奇怪的事情——神话里仙母是真碰得到的——有钱人是有心肠的,女人和女人是姊妹。她突然转过身子去,说:"不要害怕。再说,你有什么可怕的,跟我一同走有什么怕?我们都是女人。就说我的地位比你的好,你就该盼望……"

　　可是刚巧这时候,她正不知道怎样说完那句话,车子停了,铃子一按,门开了,蔷媚有她那殷勤的姿态，半保护地，简直抱着她似的，把那女子拉进了屋子去。暖和，柔软，光亮，一种甜香味儿，这在她是享惯了的平常不放在心上，这时候看还有那个怎样的领略。有意思极了的。她像是一个富人家的女孩子在她的奶房里，柜子打开一个又一个，纸盒儿放散一个又一个的。

"来，上楼来，"蔷媚说，急于要开始她的慷慨，"上来到我房间里去。"这来也好救出这可怜的小东西，否则叫下人们盯着看就够受的；她们一边走上楼梯，她心里就打算连金儿都不去按铃叫她，换衣服什么她自个儿来。顶要紧的事情是要做得自然！

"得！"蔷媚第二次又叫了，她们走到了她那宽大的卧房；窗帘全已拉拢了的，壁炉里的火光在她那套精美的水漆家具，金线的坐垫，淡黄的浅蓝的地毡上直晃耀。

那女子就在靠近门那儿站着，她看昏了的样子。可是蔷媚不介意那个。

"来坐下，"她叫，把她那大椅子拉近了火，"这椅子舒泰。来这儿暖和暖和。你一定冷极了。"

"我不敢，太太。"那女子说，她挨着往后退。

"喔，来吧，"——蔷媚跑过去——"你有什么怕的，不要怕，真的。坐下，等我脱下了我的东西我们一同到间壁屋子吃茶舒服去。为什么你怕？"她就轻轻地把那瘦小的人儿半推似的按进了她的深深的摇床。

那女子不作声。她就痴痴地坐着，一双手挂在两边，她的口微微地开着。说实话，她那样儿够蠢的。可是蔷媚她不承认那个。她靠着她的一边，问她："你脱了你的帽子不好？你的美头发全湿了的。不戴帽子舒服得多不是？"

这回她听着一声轻极了的仿佛是"好的，太太"，那顶压扁了的帽子就下来了。

"我再来帮你脱了外套吧。"蔷媚说。

那女子站了起来。可是她一手撑着椅子，就让蔷媚给拉。这可费劲了。她自个儿简直没有动活。她站都站不稳像个小孩，蔷媚的心里不由得想，一个人要旁人帮忙他自己也得稍微，就要稍微，帮衬一点才好，否则事情就为难了。现在她拿这件外套怎么办呢？她给放在地板上，帽子也一起搁着。她正在壁炉架上拿下一支烟卷来，忽然听得那女子快声地说，音是低得可有点儿怪："我对不住，太太，可是我要晕了。我得昏了，太太，要是我不吃一点东西。"

"了了不得，我怎么地糊涂！"蔷媚奔过去按铃了。

"茶！马上拿茶来！立刻要点儿白兰地！"

下女来了又去了，可是那女子简直地哭了。"不，我不，不要白兰地。我从来不喝白兰地，我要的就是一杯茶，太太。"她眼泪都来了。

这阵子是又可怕又有趣的。蔷媚跑在她椅子的一边。

"不要哭，可怜的小东西。"她说。

"别哭。"她拿她的花边手帕给她。她真的心里说不出地感动了。她把她的手臂放在那一对瘦削的鸟样的肩膀上。

这来她才心定了点儿，不怕了，什么都忘了，就知道她们俩都是女人，她咽着说："我再不能这样儿下去，我受不了这个，我再不能受。我非得自个儿了了完事，我再也受不了了。"

"你用不着的。有我顾着你。再不要哭了。

你看你碰着我还不是好事情？我们一忽儿吃茶，你有什么都对我说：我会替你想法子。我答应你。好了，不哭了。怪累的，好了！"

她果然停了，正够蔷媚站起身，茶点就来了。她移过一个桌子来放在她们中间。她这样那样什么都让给那可怜的小人儿吃，所有的夹肉饼，所有的牛油面包，她那茶杯一空就给她倒上，加奶酪，加糖。人家总说糖是滋补的。她自己没有吃；她抽她的烟，又故意眼往一边看，不叫她对面人觉着羞。

真的是，那一顿小点心的效力够奇怪的。茶桌子一挪开，一个新人儿，一个小个儿怯弱的身材，一头发揉着的，黑黑口唇，深的有光的眼，靠在那大椅子里，一种倦慵慵的神情，对壁炉里的火光望着。蔷媚又点上一支烟，这该是时候谈天了。

"你最后一餐饭是什么时候吃的？"她软软地问。

但正这时候门上的手把转动了。

"蔷媚，我可以进来吗？"是菲立伯。

"当然。"

他进来了。"喔，对不住。"他说，他停住了直望。

"你来吧，不碍，"蔷媚笑着说，"这是我的我的朋友，密斯——。"

"司密司，太太，"倦慵慵的那个说，她这忽儿倒是异常地镇定，也不怕。

"司密司，"蔷媚说，"我们正要谈点儿天哪。"

"喔，是的。""很好，"说着他的眼瞟着了地板上的外套和帽子。他走过来，背着火站着。"这下半天天时太坏了。"他留神地说，眼睛依然冲着倦慵慵的那个看，看她的手，她的鞋，然后再望着蔷媚。

"可不是，"蔷媚欣欣地说，"下流的天气！"

菲立伯笑了，他那媚人的笑。"我方才进来是要，"他说，"你跟我到书房里去一去。你可以吗？密斯司密司许我们不？"

那一对大眼睛挺了起来瞅着他，可是蔷媚替她答了话。"当然她许的。"他们俩一起出房去了。

"我说，"菲立伯到了书房里说，"讲给我听。

她是谁？这算什么意思？”

蔷媚，嘻嘻地笑着，身体靠在门上说："她是我在寇崇街上捡了来的，真的是。她是一个真正的'捡来货'。她问我要一杯的茶钱，我就带了她回家。"

"可是你想拿她怎么办呢？"

"待她好，"蔷媚快快地说，"待她稀奇地好，顾着她。我也不知道怎么了，我们还没有谈哪。可是指点她——看待她——使她觉着——"

"我的乖乖孩子，"菲立伯说，"你够发疯了，你知道。哪儿有这样办法的。"

"我知道你一定这么说，"蔷媚回驳他，"为什么不？我要这么着。那还不够理由？再说，在书上不是常念到这类事情。我决意——"

"可是，"菲立伯慢吞吞地说，割去一支雪茄的头，"她长得这十二分好看。"

"好看？"蔷媚没有防备他这一来，她脸都红了。"你说她好看？我——我没有想着。"

"真是的！"菲立伯划了一根火柴。"是简直的可爱。再看看去，我的孩子。方才我进你屋的时候，我简直看迷糊了。但是……我想你事情做错了。对不起，乖乖，如其我太粗鲁了或是什么。可是你得按时候让我知道密斯司密司跟不跟我们一起吃晚饭，我吃前还要看看衣饰杂志哪。"

"你这怪东西！"蔷媚说，她走进了书房，又不回她自己房里去，她走进他的书写间去，在他的书台边坐下了。好看！简直的可爱！看迷糊了！她的心像一个大皮球似的跳着，好看！可爱！她手拉着她那本支票簿。可是不对，支票用不着的，当然。她打开一个抽屉，拿出了五张镑票看了看，放回去两张，把那三张挤在手掌心里，她走回她卧房去了。

半小时以后菲立伯还在书房里，蔷媚进来了。

"我就来告诉你，"她说，她又靠在门上，望着他，又是她那扁眯着，眼带"洋味儿"的看法，"密斯司密司今晚不跟我们吃饭了。"

菲立伯放下了手里的报。"喔，为什么了？她另有约会？"

蔷媚过来坐在他的腿上。"她一定要走，"她说，"所以我送了那可怜人儿一点儿钱。她要去我也不能勉强她不是？"她软软地又加上一句。

蔷媚方才收拾了她的头发，微微地添深了一
点她的眼圈，也戴上了她的珠子。她伸起一双手
来，摸着菲立伯的脸。

"你喜欢我不？"她说，她那声音，甜甜的，
也有点儿发粗。

"我喜欢你极了，"他说，紧紧地抱住她，"亲
我。"

隔了一阵子。

蔷媚迷离地说："我见一只有趣的小盒儿，
要二十八个几尼哪。你许我买不？"

菲立伯在膝盖上颠着她，"许你，你这会花
钱的小东西。"他说。

可是那并不是蔷媚要说的话。

"菲立伯，"那低声地说，她拿他的头紧抵着
她的胸膛，"我好看不？"

# *A Cup of Tea*

*R*osemary Fell was not exactly beautiful. No, you couldn't have called her beautiful. Pretty? Well, if you took her to pieces... But why be so cruel as to take anyone to pieces? She was young, brilliant, extremely modern, exquisitely well dressed, amazingly well read in the newest of the new books, and her parties were the most delicious mixture of the really important people and... artists—quaint creatures, discoveries of hers, some of them too terrifying for words, but others quite presentable and amusing.

Rosemary had been married two years. She had a duck of a boy. No, not Peter—Michael. And her husband absolutely adored her. They were rich, really rich, not just comfortably well off, which is odious and stuffy and sounds like one's grandparents. But if Rosemary wanted to shop she would go to Paris as you and I would go to Bond Street. If she wanted to buy flowers, the car pulled up at that perfect shop in Regent Street, and Rosemary inside the shop just gazed in her dazzled, rather exotic way, and said, "I want those and those and those. Give me four bunches of those. And that jar of roses. Yes, I'll have all the roses in the jar. No, no lilac. I hate lilac. It's got no shape." The attendant bowed and put the lilac out of sight, as though this was only too true; lilac was dreadfully shapeless. "Give me those stumpy little tulips. Those red and white ones." And she was followed to the car by a thin shopgirl staggering under an immense white paper armful that looked like a baby in long clothes...

One winter afternoon she had been buying something in a little antique shop in Curzon Street. It was a shop she liked. For one thing, one usually had it to oneself. And then the man who kept it was ridiculously fond of serving her. He beamed whenever she came in. He clasped his hands; he was so gratified he could scarcely speak. Flattery, of course. All the same, there was something...

"You see, madam," he would explain in his low respectful tones, "I love my things. I would rather not part with them than sell them to someone who does not appreciate them, who has not that fine feeling which is so rare..." And, breathing deeply he unrolled a tiny square of blue velvet and pressed it on the glass counter with his pale finger-tips.

Today it was a little box. He had been keeping it for her. He had shown it to nobody as yet. An exquisite little enamel box with a glaze so fine it looked as though it had been baked in cream. On the lid a minute creature stood under a flowery tree, and a more minute creature still had her arms round his neck. Her hat, really no bigger than a geranium petal, hung from a branch; it had green ribbons. And there was a pink cloud like a watchful cherub floating above their heads. Rosemary took her hands out of her long gloves. She always took off her gloves to examine such things. Yes, she liked it very much.

She loved it; it was a great duck. She must have it. And, turning the creamy box, opening and shutting it, she couldn't help noticing how charming her hands were against the blue velvet. The shopman, in some dim cavern of his mind, may have dared to think so too. For he took a pencil, leant over the counter, and his pale bloodless fingers crept timidly towards those rosy, flashing ones, as he murmured gently, "If I may venture to point out to madam, the flowers on the little lady's bodice."

"Charming!" Rosemary admired the flowers. But what was the price? For a moment the shopman did not seem to hear. Then a murmur reached her. "Twenty-eight guineas, madam."

"Twenty-eight guineas." Rosemary gave no sign. She laid the little box down; she buttoned her gloves again. Twenty-eight guineas. Even if one is rich... She looked vague. She stared at a plump tea-kettle like a plump hen above the shopman's head, and her voice was dreamy as she answered, "Well, keep it for me—will you? I'll..."

But the shopman had already bowed as though keeping it for her was all any human being could ask. He would be willing, of course, to keep it for her for ever.

The discreet door shut with a click. She was outside on the step, gazing at the winter afternoon. Rain was falling, and with the rain it seemed the dark came too, spinning down like ashes. There was a cold bitter taste in the air, and the new-lighted lamps looked sad. Sad were the lights in the houses opposite. Dimly they burned as if regretting something. And people hurried by, hidden under their hateful umbrellas. Rosemary felt a strange pang. She pressed her muff against her breast; she wished she had the little box, too, to cling to. Of course, the car was there. She'd only to cross the pavement. But still she waited. There are moments, horrible moments in life, when one emerges from shelter and looks out, and it's awful. One oughtn't to give way to them. One ought to go home and have an extra-special tea. But at the very instant of thinking that, a young girl,

thin, dark, shadowy—where had she come from?—
was standing at Rosemary's elbow and a voice like
a sigh, almost like a sob, breathed, "Madam, may I
speak to you a moment?"

"Speak to me? "Rosemary turned. She saw a little
battered creature with enormous eyes, someone quite
young, no older than herself, who clutched at her
coat-collar with reddened hands, and shivered as
though she had just come out of the water.

"M-madam," stammered the voice. "Would you
let me have the price of a cup of tea?"

"A cup of tea? " There was something simple,
sincere in that voice; it wasn't in the least the voice
of a beggar. "Then have you no money at all?" asked
Rosemary.

"None, madam," came the answer.

"How extraordinary! "Rosemary peered through
the dusk, and the girl gazed back at her. How more
than extraordinary! And suddenly it seemed to
Rosemary such an adventure. It was like something
out of a novel by Dostoevsky, this meeting in the

dusk. Supposing she took the girl home? Supposing she did do one of those things she was always reading about or seeing on the stage, what would happen? It would be thrilling. And she heard herself saying afterwards to the amazement of her friends, "I simply took her home with me," as she stepped forward and said to that dim person beside her, "Come home to tea with me."

The girl drew back startled. She even stopped shivering for a moment. Rosemary put out a hand and touched her arm. "I mean it," she said, smiling. And she felt how simple and kind her smile was. "Why won't you? Do. Come home with me now in my car and have tea."

"You—you don't mean it, madam," said the girl, and there was pain in her voice.

"But I do," cried Rosemary. "I want you to. To please me. Come along."

The girl put her fingers to her lips and her eyes devoured Rosemary. "You're—you're not taking me to the police station? " she stammered.

"The police station! " Rosemary laughed out. "Why should I be so cruel? No, I only want to make you warm and to hear— anything you care to tell me."

Hungry people are easily led. The footman held the door of the car open, and a moment later they were skimming through the dusk.

"There! "said Rosemary. She had a feeling of triumph as she slipped her hand through the velvet strap. She could have said, "Now I've got you," as she gazed at the little captive she had netted. But of course she meant it kindly. Oh, more than kindly. She was going to prove to this girl that—wonderful things did happen in life, that—fairy godmothers were real, that— rich people had hearts, and that women were sisters. She turned impulsively, saying, "Don't be frightened. After all, why shouldn't you come back with me? We're both women. If I'm the more fortunate, you ought to expect..."

But happily at that moment, for she didn't know how the sentence was going to end, the car stopped.

The bell was rung, the door opened, and with a charming, protecting, almost embracing movement, Rosemary drew the other into the hall. Warmth, softness, light, a sweet scent, all those things so familiar to her she never even thought about them, she watched that other receive. It was fascinating. She was like the rich little girl in her nursery with all the cupboards to open, all the boxes to unpack.

"Come, come upstairs," said Rosemary, longing to begin to be generous. "Come up to my room." And, besides, she wanted to spare this poor little thing from being stared at by the servants; she decided as they mounted the stairs she would not even ring for Jeanne, but take off her things by herself. The great thing was to be natural!

And "There! " cried Rosemary again, as they reached her beautiful big bedroom with the curtains drawn, the fire leaping on her wonderful lacquer furniture, her gold cushions and the primrose and blue rugs.

The girl stood just inside the door; she seemed

dazed. But Rosemary didn't mind that.

"Come and sit down," she cried, dragging her big chair up to the fire, "in this comfy chair. Come and get warm. You look so dreadfully cold."

"I daren't, madam," said the girl, and she edged backwards.

"Oh, please,"—Rosemary ran forward—" you mustn't be frightened, you mustn't, really. Sit down, and when I've taken off my things we shall go into the next room and have tea and be cosy. Why are you afraid? "And gently she half pushed the thin figure into its deep cradle.

But there was no answer. The girl stayed just as she had been put, with her hands by her sides and her mouth slightly open. To be quite sincere, she looked rather stupid. But Rosemary wouldn't acknowledge it. She leant over her, saying, "Won't you take off your hat? Your pretty hair is all wet. And one is so much more comfortable without a hat, isn't one? "

There was a whisper that sounded like "Very good, madam," and the crushed hat was taken off.

"And let me help you off with your coat, too," said Rosemary.

The girl stood up. But she held on to the chair with one hand and let Rosemary pull. It was quite an effort. The other scarcely helped her at all. She seemed to stagger like a child, and the thought came and went through Rosemary's mind, that if people wanted helping they must respond a little, just a little, otherwise it became very difficult indeed. And what was she to do with the coat now? She left it on the floor, and the hat too. She was just going to take a cigarette off the mantelpiece when the girl said quickly, but so lightly and strangely, "I'm very sorry, madam, but I'm going to faint. I shall go off, madam, if I don't have something."

"Good heavens, how thoughtless I am! " Rosemary rushed to the bell.

"Tea! Tea at once! And some brandy immediately! "

The maid was gone again, but the girl almost cried out. "No, I don't want no brandy. I never drink brandy. It's a cup of tea I want, madam." And she burst into tears.

It was a terrible and fascinating moment. Rosemary knelt beside her chair.

"Don't cry, poor little thing," she said. "Don't cry." And she gave the other her lace handkerchief. She really was touched beyond words. She put her arm round those thin, bird-like shoulders.

Now at last the other forgot to be shy, forgot everything except that they were both women, and gasped out, "I can't go on no longer like this. I can't bear it. I can't bear it. I shall do away with myself. I can't bear no more."

"You shan't have to. I'll look after you. Don't cry any more. Don't you see what a good thing it was that you met me? We'll have tea and you'll tell me everything. And I shall arrange something. I promise. Do stop crying. It's so exhausting. Please!"

The other did stop just in time for Rosemary to get up before the tea came. She had the table placed between them. She plied the poor little creature with everything, all the sandwiches, all the bread and butter, and every time her cup was empty she filled it with tea, cream and sugar. People always said sugar was so nourishing. As for herself she didn't eat; she smoked and looked away tactfully so that the other should not be shy.

And really the effect of that slight meal was marvellous. When the tea-table was carried away a new being, a light, frail creature with tangled hair, dark lips, deep, lighted eyes, lay back in the big chair in a kind of sweet languor, looking at the blaze. Rosemary lit a fresh cigarette; it was time to begin.

"And when did you have your last meal? " she asked softly.

But at that moment the door-handle turned.

"Rosemary, may I come in? " It was Philip.

"Of course."

He came in. "Oh, I'm so sorry," he said, and stopped and stared.

"It's quite all right," said Rosemary smiling. "This is my friend, Miss——"

"Smith, madam," said the languid figure, who was

strangely still and unafraid.

"Smith," said Rosemary. "We are going to have a little talk."

"Oh, yes," said Philip. "Quite," and his eyes caught sight of the coat and hat on the floor. He came over to the fire and turned his back to it. "It's a beastly afternoon," he said curiously, still looking at that listless figure, looking at its hands and boots, and then at Rosemary again.

"Yes, isn't it? " said Rosemary enthusiastically. "Vile! "

Philip smiled his charming smile. "As a matter of fact," said he, "I wanted you to come into the library for a moment. Would you? Will Miss Smith excuse us! "

The big eyes were raised to him, but Rosemary answered for her. "Of course she will." And they went out of the room together.

"I say," said Philip, when they were alone. "Explain. Who is she? What does it all mean?"

Rosemary, laughing, leaned against the door and

said, "I picked her up in Curzon Street. Really. She's a real pick-up. She asked me for the price of a cup of tea, and I brought her home with me."

"But what on earth are you going to do with her? " cried Philip.

"Be nice to her," said Rosemary quickly. "Be frightfully nice to her. Look after her. I don't know how. We haven't talked yet. But show her—treat her—make her feel——" "My darling girl," said Philip, "you're quite mad, you know. It simply can't be done."

"I knew you'd say that," retorted Rosemary. "Why not? I want to. Isn't that a reason? And besides, one's always reading about these things. I decided——"

"But," said Philip slowly, and he cut the end of a cigar, "she's so astonishingly pretty."

"Pretty? " Rosemary was so surprised that she blushed. "Do you think so? I—I hadn't thought about it."

"Good Lord! " Philip struck a match. "She's absolutely lovely. Look again, my child. I was bowled over when I came into your room just now. However... I think you're making a ghastly mistake. Sorry, darling, if I'm crude and all that. But let me know if Miss Smith is going to dine with us in time for me to look up The Milliner's Gazette."

"You absurd creature! " said Rosemary, and she went out of the library, but not back to her bedroom. She went to her writing-room and sat down at her desk. Pretty! Absolutely lovely! Bowled over! Her heart beat like a heavy ball. Pretty! Lovely! She drew her cheque-book towards her. But no, cheques would be no use, of course. She opened a drawer and took out five pound notes, looked at them, put two back, and holding the three squeezed in her hand, she went back to her bedroom.

Half an hour later Philip was still in the library, when Rosemary came in.

"I only wanted to tell you," said she, and she leaned against the door again and looked at him with her dazzled exotic gaze, "Miss Smith won't dine with us tonight."

Philip put down the paper. "Oh, what's happened? Previous engagement?"

Rosemary came over and sat down on his knee. "She insisted on going," said she, "so I gave the poor little thing a present of money. I couldn't keep her against her will, could I?" she added softly.

Rosemary had just done her hair, darkened her eyes a little, and put on her pearls. She put up her hands and touched Philip's cheeks.

"Do you like me? "said she, and her tone, sweet, husky, troubled him.

"I like you awfully," he said, and he held her tighter. "Kiss me."

There was a pause.

Then Rosemary said dreamily. "I saw a fascinating little box to-day. It cost twenty-eight guineas. May I have it?"

Philip jumped her on his knee. "You may, little wasteful one," said he.

But that was not really what Rosemary wanted to say.

"Philip," she whispered, and she pressed his head against her bosom. "Am I pretty? "

# 巴克妈妈的行状

巴克妈妈是替一个独身的文学家收拾屋子的。一天早上那文学家替她开门的时候，他问起巴克妈妈的小外孙儿。巴克妈妈站在那间暗暗的小外房的门席子上，伸出手去帮着他关了门，再答话。"我们昨天把他埋了，先生。"她静静地说。

"啊啊！我听着难过。"那文学家惊讶地说。他正在吃他的早饭。他穿着一件破烂的便袍，一张烂破的报纸，拿在一只手里。但是他觉得不好意思。要不再说一两句话，他不好意思走回他的暖和的"起坐间"去——总得再有一两句话。他想起了他们一班人下葬是看得很重的，他就和善地说，"我料想下葬办得好好儿的。"

"怎么说呢，先生？"老巴克妈妈嘎着嗓子说。

可怜的老婆子！她看得怪寒碜的。"我猜想

你们下葬办得——办得很妥当吧？"他说。巴克
妈妈没有答话。她低着头，蹒跚着走到厨间里去
了，手里抓紧着她的老旧的鱼袋，那袋里放着她
的收拾的家伙，一条厨裙，一双软皮鞋。文学家
挺了挺他的眉毛，走回他的房里吃早饭去了。

"太难受了，想是。"他高声地说着，伸手去
捞了一块橘酱。

巴克妈妈从她帽子里拔出了两支长簪，把帽
子挂在门背后。她也解开了她破旧的短外衣的衣
扣，也挂上了。她捆上了她的厨裙，坐下来脱她
的皮靴。脱皮靴或是穿皮靴是她一件苦楚的事，
但是她吃这苦楚也有好几年了。其实，她真是吃
惯这苦的，每次她连靴带都不曾解散，她的脸子
早已拉得长长的，扭得弯弯的，准备那一阵的抽
痛。换好了鞋，她叹了口气坐了下去，轻轻地抚
摸她的膝部……

"奶奶！奶奶！"她的小孙儿穿着有扣的小
皮靴站在她的衣兜上。他方才从街里玩过了进
来的。

"看，孩子，你把你的奶奶的裙子踹得像个
什么样子！你顽皮的孩子！"

但是他用一双小手臂抱着她的头项，把他的小脸子紧紧地贴着她的。

"奶奶，给我一个铜子！"他讨好地说。

"去你的，孩子；奶奶没有铜子。"

"你有的。"

"不，我没有。"

她已经伸手去摸她的破旧的，压坏的，黑皮的钱包。

"可是孩子你又有什么东西给你的奶奶呢？"他给了一个怕羞的小小的笑靥，小脸子挨得更紧了。她觉得他的眼睫毛在她的腮边跳动着。"我没有什么东西。"他喃喃地说……

老妇人跳了起来，伸手从汽油炉上拿下了铁水壶，走到废物槽边盛水去。开水壶里的沸响好像呆钝了她的心痛似的。她又装满了提桶和洗器盆的水。

没有一本整本的书，也描写不了那厨房的情形。每星期除了星期日那文学家"总算"是自己收拾的。他把用过的茶叶尽朝尽晚地倒在一个梅酱瓶里，那是放着专为倒茶叶用的，要是他用完了干净的叉子，就在拉得动的擦手布上篦了一个两个暂时使用。除此以外，他对他的朋友说，他的"系统"是很简单的，他总不懂人家管家就有那么多的麻烦。

"你把你所有的家具全使脏了，每星期叫一个老婆子来替你收拾不就完？"

结果是把厨房弄成了一个巨大的垃圾桶。连地板上满是面包皮屑，信封，烟卷蒂头。但是巴克妈妈倒不怨他。她看这年轻的先生没有人看着他，怪可怜的。从那烟煤熏黑了的窗子望出去只看见一大片惨淡的天，有时天上起了云，那些云也看得像用旧了，老惫了似的，边上擦烂了的，中间有的是破洞，或是用过了茶叶似的暗点子。

一面壶里的水在蒸汽，巴克妈妈拿了帚子扫地。"是的，"她心里想，帚子在地板上碰着，"管他长的短的，我总算有了我的份儿了。我只是劳苦了一辈子。"

就是邻居们也是这么地说她。好几回她拿着她的旧鱼袋，蹒跚着走回家的时候，她听他们站在路的转角儿上，或是靠在他们门外的铁栏子上，在说着她，"她真是劳苦了一辈子，巴克妈妈真是劳苦了一辈子。"这话真是实在的情形，所以巴克妈妈听了也没有什么得意。好比你说她是住在二十七号屋子的地层的后背，一样地不稀奇。劳苦了一辈子！……

十六岁那年她离了斯德辣脱福特，到伦敦做人家厨下帮忙的。是呀，她是生长在阿房河上的斯德辣脱福特的。莎士比亚，先生你问谁呀？不，人家常在问着她莎士比亚这样那样的。但是她却从没有听见过他的名字，直到他后来见了戏馆外面的招贴。

她的本乡她什么都记不得了，除了"黄昏时候坐在家里火炉边，从烟筒里望得见天上的明星"，还有"娘总有一长条的咸肉挂在天花板上的"。还有一点什么——一个草堆儿，有的是——在家门口儿，草香味儿顶好闻。但是那草堆儿也记不清了。就是有一两次生了病睡在病院里的时候，她记起了那门前的草堆儿。

她第一次做工的人家，是一个很凶的地方，他们从不准她出门。她也从不上楼去，除了早上与晚上的祷告。那地层倒是很整齐的。厨娘待她也很凶。她常抢她没有看过的家信，掷在火灶里毁了，因为怪她看了信总是做梦似的想心事……

还有那些蟑螂！你许不信——她没有到伦敦之
前，从没有见过一个黑偷油婆儿。每次讲到这儿
巴克妈妈总是自己要笑的，好像是……从没有见
过一个黑偷油婆儿！得了！这不是比如说你从没
有见过你自个儿的脚，一样地可笑。

后来这家人家把房子卖了，她又到一个医
生家里去"帮忙"，在那里做了两年早上忙到晚
的工以后，她就和她的男人结婚。他是一个面
包师。

"他是做面包的，巴克太太！"那文学家就
说。因为有时候他也暂时放下他的书本，留心来
听她的讲话，讲她的——生平。"嫁一个面包师
准是顶有意思的！"

巴克太太的神气没有他那样的有把握。

"这样洁净的生意。"文学家说。

巴克太太还是不大相信。

"你不愿意把新鲜做出来的整块的面包，递
给你们的主顾吗？"

"可是，先生，"巴克妈妈说，"我老在地层
里，不大上楼到店里去。我们总共有十三个小
孩，七个已经埋了。我们的家要不是医院，就是

病院，对不对呢？”

“真的是，巴克太太！”文学家说着，耸着肩膀，又把笔拿在手里了。

是的，七个已经去了，剩下的六个还不曾长大，她的丈夫得了肺病，那是面粉入肺，那时医生告诉她……她的丈夫坐在床里，衬衫从后背翻上头，医生的指头在他的背上画了一个圆圈。

“我说，要是我们把他从这里打开，巴克太太，”那医生说，“你就看得见他的肺让白面粉打了一个大洞。呼气试试，我的好朋友！”这儿巴克太太说不清是她亲眼见的或是她的幻想，她见她可怜的丈夫口唇一开就有风车似的一阵白灰冒了出来……

但是她还得奋斗着养大她的六个小孩子，还得奋斗着自个儿过自个儿的活，可怕的奋斗！后来，等到那群孩子稍微长大一点可以上学堂去了，她丈夫的姊妹来伴他们住着帮一点子忙，可是她住不满两个月，她就从楼梯上闪了下来，伤了她的背梁。那五年内巴克妈妈又有了一个孩子——又是一个哭哭啼啼的！——她还得自个儿喂奶。后来玛蒂那孩子没有走正道儿，连着她妹子阿丽司都被带坏了；两个男孩子上了外洋，小杰姆到印度当兵去，最小的安粟嫁了一个一事无成的小堂倌，来义生的那年他生烂疮死了。现在小来义我的小外孙儿……

一堆堆的脏杯子，脏盘子，都已洗过，擦干了。墨水似的黑的刀子，先用一片白薯狠劲地擦，再用软木，才擦得干净。桌子已经擦净，食器架与那水槽子一根根沙田鱼的尾巴在泳着……

那孩子从小就不强健——从小就是的。他长得怯怜怜的，人家看了都当是女孩子。银白的好看的发卷儿他有，小蓝眼儿，鼻子的一边有宝石似的一个小斑点儿。养大那孩子，她与她女儿安粟费的劲儿！报上有什么，她们就买了让他读！每星期日的早上安粟高声地念报，一面巴克妈妈洗她的衣服。

"好先生，——我就写一行字让你知道我的小孩梅的儿差不多已经死了……用了你的药四瓶……在九星期内长了八磅的重，现在还在继续地加重哪。"

念了这类的药广告，架子上盛着墨水的鸡蛋杯就拿了下来，买药的信也写成了，明天早上妈妈去做工的时候乘便就到邮局里去买了一张邮汇单。但是还是没有用。什么法子都不能叫小来义加重。就是带了他到惨淡的墓园去，他的小脸子上也比不出一点活泼的颜色，老是那青白的；就是抱了他去坐街车好好地震他一次，回家来他的胃口还是不成。

但是他是奶奶的孩子，原先就是的……

"你是谁的孩子呀？"巴克妈妈说着，伸着腰，从炉灶边走到烟煤熏黑的窗边去了。一个小孩的口音，又亲热，又密切，妈妈几乎气都喘不过来——那小口音好像就在她的胸口，在她的心里——笑了出来，喊说，"我是奶奶的孩子！"

正在那个时候来了一阵脚步声，文学家已经穿了衣服预备出门散步去。

"巴克太太，我出去了。"

"是您哪，先生。"

"你的'二先令六'我放在墨水架的小盘上。"

"费心您哪，先生。"

"啊，我倒想起了，巴克太太，"文学家急促地说，"上次你在这儿的时候，有些可可你没有掷了吗?"

"没有,先生。"

"很怪,明明的有一调羹的可可剩在铁筒子里的,赌咒都成。"他转身走了。他又回头说,和缓地,坚定地,"以后你要掷了什么东西,请你告诉我一声,好不好,巴克太太?"他走了开去,很得意的神气,他自以为他已经让巴克太太明白,别看他样子不精明。他同女太太们一样的细心哪。

"嘭"的一声门关上了。她拿了她的刷子,揩抹布,到卧房里去收拾,但是她在铺床的时候,拉直着,折拢着,轻拍着,她还是忘不了她的小外孙儿,她想着真难受。为什么他要那样地受罪?她总是想不通。为什么一个好好的安琪儿似的小孩,会得连喘气都得同人要,用得着吃那样的大苦。要一个小孩子遭那样的大罪,她看得真没有意思。

……来义的小胸膛发出一种声响,像是水在壶滚沸似的。有一大块的东西老是在他的胸膛里泛泡似的,他怎么也摆脱不了。他一咳嗽,汗就在他的头上钻了出来;他的眼也胀大了,手也震着，他胸口里的一大块就在那里泛泡，像一个白薯在锅子里乱滚似的。这还不算什么，最难受的是他有时也不咳嗽，他就是背着枕头坐着，不说话也不答话，有时竟是连话都听不见似的。他就是坐着，满面的不痛快。

"这可不是你的可怜的老奶奶的不好，我的乖乖。"老巴克妈妈说，在他涨紫了的小耳朵边轻掠着他汗湿了的头发。但是来义摇着他的头，避开了去，看得像是和她很过不去似的——脸子还是沉沉的。他低着他的头，斜着眼望着她，像是他不能相信这是他的奶奶似的。

但是到了末了……巴克妈妈把压床被甩着，铺过床去。不，她简直地想都不能想。

这是太难了——她一生的命实在是太苦了。她一直忍耐到今天，她，她还得自己顾管自己，也从没有人见她哭过。谁都没有见过，就是她自己的孩子也从没有见过她倒下来。可是现在！来义完了——她还有什么？她什么都完了。她过了一辈子就是淘成了一个他，现在他也没有了。为什么这些个儿事情全碰着我？她倒要问。"我做了什么事？"老妈妈说，"我做了什么事？"

她一头说着话，她手里的刷子掉了下去。她已经在厨间里。她心里难受得可怕，她就戴上了她的帽子，穿上了外衣，走出了那屋子，像在梦里似的。她自己也不明白她在干什么。她像是一个人让什么可怕的事吓疯了转身就跑似的——哪儿都好，只要走开了就像是逃出了……

那时街上很冷，风来像冰似的，来往的人快步地走着，很快；男人走着像剪子，女人像猫。没有人知道——也没有人管。就使她倒了下来就便隔了这么多的年份，到底她哭了出来，她着落在那儿呢——拘留所，也许的。

但是她一想着哭，就像小来义跳上了他奶奶的臂膀似的。啊，她就想哭，小团团。奶奶要哭。只要她现在哭得出，一场痛痛快快地大哭，什么都该得哭，一直从她初次做工的地方与那凶恶的厨娘哭起，哭过去哭到第二次做工的那医生家里，再哭那七个早死的小的，再哭她丈夫的死，再哭她走散了的孩子们，再哭以后苦恼的日子，一直哭到小外孙儿来义。但是要认真的什么都得哭，一件件地哭，就得有多大的工夫。还是一样，哭的时候已经到了。她总得哭一场。她再不能放着等；她再不能等了……她能上哪儿去呢？

"她是劳苦了一生的，巴克太太。"是的，劳苦了一生，真是！她的腮子颤动起来了；要去就得去了。但是哪儿呢？哪儿呢？

她不能回家，安粟在那儿，她准把安粟的命都吓跑了。她不能随便选一个路凳坐着哭：人家准会过来盘问她。她又不能回到她那先生的屋子去；她不能在旁人的家里放着嗓子号哭。要是她坐在露天的阶沿石级上，就有警察过来对她说话。

啊，难道真是连一个可以自个儿躲起来随她爱待多久，不麻烦人家，也没有人来"别扭"她的地方都找不到了吗？难道真是在这世界上就没有她可以尽性地哭他一个痛快的地方了吗——到底？

巴克妈妈站定了，向天望望，向地望望：冰冷的风吹着她的厨裙，卷成了一个气球。现在天又下雨了。还是没有地方去。

## *Life of Ma Parker*

When the literary gentleman, whose flat old Ma Parker cleaned every Tuesday, opened the door to her that morning, he asked after her grandson. Ma Parker stood on the doormat inside the dark little hall, and she stretched out her hand to help her gentleman shut the door before she replied. "We buried 'im yesterday, sir," she said quietly.

"Oh, dear me! I'm sorry to hear that," said the literary gentleman in a shocked tone. He was in the middle of his breakfast. He wore a very shabby dressing-gown and carried a crumpled newspaper in one hand. But he felt awkward. He could hardly go back to the warm sitting-room without saying something—something more. Then because these people set such store by funerals he said kindly, "I hope the funeral went off all right."

"Beg parding, sir?" said old Ma Parker huskily.

Poor old bird! She did look dashed. "I hope the funeral was a—a—success," said he. Ma Parker gave no answer. She bent her head and hobbled off to the kitchen, clasping the old fish bag that held her cleaning things and an apron and a pair of felt shoes. The literary gentleman raised his eyebrows and went back to his breakfast.

"Overcome, I suppose," he said aloud, helping himself to the marmalade.

Ma Parker drew the two jetty spears out of her toque and hung it behind the door. She unhooked her worn jacket and hung that up too. Then she tied her apron and sat down to take off her boots. To take off her boots or to put them on was an agony to her, but it had been an agony for years. In fact, she was so accustomed to the pain that her face was drawn and screwed up ready for the twinge before she'd so much as untied the laces. That over, she sat back with a sigh and softly rubbed her knees...

"Gran! Gran!" Her little grandson stood on her lap in his button boots. He'd just come in from playing in the street.

"Look what a state you've made your gran's skirt into—you wicked boy!"

But he put his arms round her neck and rubbed his cheek against hers.

"Gran, gi' us a penny!" he coaxed.

"Be off with you; Gran ain't got no pennies."

"Yes, you 'ave."

"No, I ain't."

"Yes, you 'ave. Gi' us one!"

Already she was feeling for the old, squashed, black leather purse.

"Well, what'll you give your gran?"

He gave a shy little laugh and pressed closer. She felt his eyelid quivering against her cheek. "I ain't got nothing," he murmured...

The old woman sprang up, seized the iron kettle off the gas stove and took it over to the sink. The noise of the water drumming in the kettle deadened her pain, it seemed. She filled the pail, too, and the washing-up bowl.

It would take a whole book to describe the state of that kitchen. During the week the literary gentleman "did" for himself. That is to say, he emptied the tea leaves now and again into a jam jar set aside for that purpose, and if he ran out of clean forks he wiped over one or two on the roller towel. Otherwise, as he explained to his friends, his "system" was quite simple, and he couldn't understand why people made all this fuss about housekeeping.

"You simply dirty everything you've got, get a hag in once a week to clean up, and the thing's done."

The result looked like a gigantic dustbin. Even the floor was littered with toast crusts, envelopes, cigarette ends. But Ma Parker bore him no grudge. She pitied the poor young gentleman for having no one to look after him. Out of the smudgy little window you could see an immense expanse of sad-looking sky, and whenever there were clouds they looked very worn, old clouds, frayed at the edges, with holes in them, or dark stains like tea.

While the water was heating, Ma Parker began sweeping the floor. "Yes," she thought, as the broom knocked, "what with one thing and another I've had my share. I've had a hard life."

Even the neighbours said that of her. Many a time, hobbling home with her fish bag she heard them, waiting at the corner, or leaning over the area railings, say among themselves, "She's had a hard life, has Ma Parker." And it was so true she wasn't in the least proud of it. It was just as if you were to say she lived in the basement-back at Number 27. A hard life!...

At sixteen she'd left Stratford and come up to London as kitching-maid. Yes, she was born in Stratford-upon-Avon. Shakespeare, sir? No, people were always arsking her about him. But she'd never heard his name until she saw it on the theatres.

Nothing remained of Stratford except that "sitting in the fire-place of a evening you could see the stars through the chimley", and "Mother always 'ad 'er side of bacon, 'anging from the ceiling." And there was something—a bush, there was—at the front door, that smelt ever so nice. But the bush was very vague. She'd only remembered it once or twice in the hospital, when she'd been taken bad.

That was a dreadful place—her first place. She was never allowed out. She never went upstairs except for prayers morning and evening. It was a fair cellar. And the cook was a cruel woman. She used to snatch away her letters from home before she'd read them, and throw them in the range because they made her dreamy... And the beedles! Would you believe it?—until she came to London she'd never seen a black beedle. Here Ma always gave a little laugh, as though—not to have seen a black beedle! Well! It was as if to say you'd never seen your own feet.

When that family was sold up she went as "help" to a doctor's house, and after two years there, on the run from morning till night, she married her husband.

He was a baker.

"A baker, Mrs. Parker!" the literary gentleman would say. For occasionally he laid aside his tomes and lent an ear, at least, to this product called Life. "It must be rather nice to be married to a baker!"

Mrs. Parker didn't look so sure.

"Such a clean trade," said the gentleman.

Mrs. Parker didn't look convinced.

"And didn't you like handing the new loaves to the customers?"

"Well, sir," said Mrs. Parker, "I wasn't in the shop above a great deal. We had thirteen little ones and buried seven of them. If it wasn't the 'ospital it was the infirmary, you might say!"

"You might, indeed, Mrs. Parker!" said the gentleman, shuddering, and taking up his pen again.

Yes, seven had gone, and while the six were still small her husband was taken ill with consumption. It was flour on the lungs, the doctor told her at the time... Her husband sat up in bed with his shirt pulled over his head, and the doctor's finger drew a circle on his back.

"Now, if we were to cut him open here, Mrs. Parker," said the doctor, "you'd find his lungs chock-a-block with white powder. Breathe, my good fellow!" And Mrs. Parker never knew for certain whether she saw or whether she fancied she saw a great fan of white dust come out of her poor dead husband's lips...

But the struggle she'd had to bring up those six little children and keep herself to herself. Terrible it had been! Then, just when they were old enough to go to school her husband's sister came to stop with them to help things along, and she hadn't been there more than two months when she fell down a flight of steps and hurt her spine. And for five years Ma Parker had another baby—and such a one for crying!—to look after. Then young Maudie went wrong and took her sister Alice with her; the two boys emigrated, and young Jim went to India with the army, and Ethel, the youngest, married a good-for-nothing little waiter who died of ulcers the year little Lennie was born. And now little Lennie—my grandson...

The piles of dirty cups, dirty dishes, were washed and dried. The ink-black knives were cleaned with a piece of potato and finished off with a piece of cork. The table was scrubbed, and the dresser and the sink that had sardine tails swimming in it...

He'd never been a strong child—never from the first. He'd been one of those fair babies that everybody took for a girl. Silvery fair curls he had, blue eyes, and a little freckle like a diamond on one side of his nose. The trouble she and Ethel had had to rear that child! The things out of the newspapers they tried him with! Every Sunday morning Ethel would read aloud while Ma Parker did her washing.

"Dear Sir,—Just a line to let you know my little Myrtil was laid out for dead... After four bottles... gained 8 lbs. in 9 weeks, and is still putting it on."

And then the egg-cup of ink would come off the dresser and the letter would be written, and Ma would buy a postal order on her way to work next

morning. But it was no use. Nothing made little
Lennie put it on. Taking him to the cemetery, even,
never gave him a colour; a nice shake-up in the bus
never improved his appetite.

But he was gran's boy from the first...

"Whose boy are you?" said old Ma Parker,
straightening up from the stove and going over to
the smudgy window. And a little voice, so warm, so
close, it half stifled her—it seemed to be in her breast
under her heart—laughed out, and said, "I'm gran's
boy!"

At that moment there was a sound of steps, and
the literary gentleman appeared, dressed for walking.

"Oh, Mrs. Parker, I'm going out."

"Very good, sir."

"And you'll find your half-crown in the tray of the
inkstand."

"Thank you, sir."

"Oh, by the way, Mrs. Parker," said the literary
gentleman quickly, "you didn't throw away any
cocoa last time you were here—did you?"

"No, sir." "Very strange. I could have sworn I left a teaspoonful of cocoa in the tin." He broke off. He said softly and firmly, "You'll always tell me when you throw things away—won't you, Mrs. Parker?" And he walked off very well pleased with himself, convinced, in fact, he'd shown Mrs. Parker that under his apparent carelessness he was as vigilant as a woman.

The door banged. She took her brushes and cloths into the bedroom. But when she began to make the bed, smoothing, tucking, patting, the thought of little Lennie was unbearable. Why did he have to suffer so? That's what she couldn't understand. Why should a little angel child have to ask for his breath and fight for it? There was no sense in making a child suffer like that.

... From Lennie's little box of a chest there came a sound as though something was boiling. There was a great lump of something bubbling in his chest that he couldn't get rid of. When he coughed the sweat sprang out on his head; his eyes bulged, his hands waved, and the great lump bubbled as a potato knocks in a saucepan. But what was more awful than all was when he didn't cough he sat against the pillow and never spoke or answered, or even made as if he heard. Only he looked offended.

"It's not your poor old gran's doing it, my lovey," said old Ma Parker, patting back the damp hair from his little scarlet ears. But Lennie moved his head and edged away. Dreadfully offended with her he looked—and solemn. He bent his head and looked at her sideways as though he couldn't have believed it of his gran.

But at the last... Ma Parker threw the counterpane over the bed. No, she simply couldn't think about it. It was too much—she'd had too much in her life to bear. She'd borne it up till now, she'd kept herself to herself, and never once had she been seen to cry. Never by a living soul. Not even her own children had seen Ma break down. She'd kept a proud face always. But now! Lennie gone—what had she? She had nothing. He was all she'd got from life, and now he was took too. Why must it all have happened to me? she wondered. "What have I done?" said old Ma Parker. "What have I done?"

As she said those words she suddenly let fall her brush. She found herself in the kitchen. Her misery was so terrible that she pinned on her hat, put on her jacket and walked out of the flat like a person in a dream. She did not know what she was doing. She was like a person so dazed by the horror of what has happened that he walks away—anywhere, as though by walking away he could escape...

It was cold in the street. There was a wind like ice. People went flitting by, very fast; the men walked like scissors; the women trod like cats. And nobody knew—nobody cared. Even if she broke down, if at last, after all these years, she were to cry, she'd find herself in the lock-up as like as not.

But at the thought of crying it was as though little Lennie leapt in his gran's arms. Ah, that's what she wants to do, my dove. Gran wants to cry. If she could only cry now, cry for a long time, over everything, beginning with her first place and the cruel cook, going on to the doctor's, and then the seven little ones, death of her husband, the children's leaving her, and all the years of misery that led up to Lennie. But to have a proper cry over all these things would take a long time. All the same, the time for it had come. She must do it. She couldn't put it off any longer; she couldn't wait any more... Where could she go?

"She's had a hard life, has Ma Parker." Yes, a hard life, indeed! Her chin began to tremble; there was no time to lose. But where? Where?

She couldn't go home; Ethel was there. It would frighten Ethel out of her life. She couldn't sit on a bench anywhere; people would come asking her questions. She couldn't possibly go back to the gentleman's flat; she had no right to cry in strangers' houses. If she sat on some steps a policeman would speak to her.

Oh, wasn't there anywhere where she could hide and keep herself to herself and stay as long as she liked, not disturbing anybody, and nobody worrying her? Wasn't there anywhere in the world where she could have her cry out—at last?

Ma Parker stood, looking up and down. The icy wind blew out her apron into a balloon. And now it began to rain. There was nowhere.

# 一个理想的家庭

　　那天下午老倪扶先生挨出了（他公司的）旋门，步下三道的石级，踏上边道，迎着满街的春意，才知道，生平第一遭，他的确是老了。——老不禁春了，春，又暖和，又殷勤，又匆忙的春，已经来了，吹弄他的白须，温存地搂着他的臂腕，他却是对付不了，他如今老了，再不能拉整衣襟，向前迈步，青年的飒爽，他没有了，他是乏了，那时晚照虽浓，他却觉得寒噤遍体。

　　霎时间他没有了精力，他再没有精神来对付明畅活泼的春，春情转把他缠糊涂了。他想止步不前，想用手杖来挥散春光，想喝一声："走你们的！"霎时间他没有了精力，就是一路照例地招呼，用手杖来轻点着帽沿，招呼一路的朋友，相识，店伙，邮差，车役，他亦觉得老大不自在。他往常心里爽快时，喜笑的斜瞬总连着殷勤的手势，仿佛说："别看我老，我比你们谁都强些。"——如今他连这一比一瞬都办不了了。他跟跄地走着，把膝部提得高高的，仿佛他在走过的空气，像水般变重了变成实质了似的，那时正值散市，一路匆匆的满是归家的人，街车不住地郎当，小车不住地切嚓，汽车摇着巨大的躯体，滚旋地前进，那样漫不经心地冲窜，只是梦想的。

那天在公司里，一切如常，没有发生什么事，海乐尔饭后到将近四点才回。他哪里去了呢？他干什么来了？他不去让他爹知道。老倪扶先生碰巧在前廊送客，海乐尔荡着大步进来了，老是他那神气，从容，娴雅，唇边挂着他那最讨女人喜欢似笑非笑的笑。

啊！海乐尔太漂亮了，实在是太漂亮了，种种的麻烦就为的是那个。男子就不应该有那样的眼，那样的睫，那样的口唇，真的怪。他的娘，他的姊妹，家里的仆役，简直把他神而明之捧；他们崇拜海乐尔，什么事都饶恕他；他从十三岁起就不老实，那年偷了他娘的钱包，拿了钱，把空钱包藏在厨子的房里。

老倪扶先生走着，想起了他，不觉狠狠地把

手杖捶着地走道的边儿。他又回想海乐尔也不单
让家里人给宠坏了，不，他的坏什么人都有份，
他只要对人一看一笑，人家就会跑到他的跟前，
所以无怪他竟整个的公司也着他的魔，哼，哼！
那可不成，做生意不是闹着玩，就是根底打稳准
发财的大公司，也不能让闹着玩，要做生意，就
得一心一意去做，要不然什么好生意都会当着眼
前失败；可是一面夏罗同女孩子们整天地嬲着
他！要他把生意整个交给海乐尔，要他息着，享
自己的福，自个儿享福！老倪扶先生越想越恼，
索性在政府大楼外面那堆棕树下呆着不走了！自
个儿享福！晚风正摇着黑沉沉的叶子，轻轻地在
咯嘎作响。好，叫他坐在家里，对着大拇指不管
事，眼看一生的事业，在海乐尔秀美的手指缝里
溜跑，消散，临了整个儿完事，一面海乐尔在
笑……

爹呀，你为什么不讲理？真是完全地用不
着，你天天地到公司去。人家见了你反而笑话你
老态，说你神气看得多倦，这不是让我们也不好
意思吗？这儿有的是大房子，花园。还不会自个
儿享福，单就生活换个样儿，也就有意思不是？

要不然你就来一样嗜好，消遣也好。

　　老腊那孩子就提起嗓子唱了进来，"谁都得有点儿嗜好，要不然就过不了活。"

　　得，得！他忍不住恶狠狠地笑了，一面他使着狠劲，在爬那小山，过了小山就是哈各德大路。他要是有了嗜好，夏罗和老腊那群孩子，便怎么办？他倒要问问。嗜好付不了房租，付不了海边的避暑，付不了她的马，她们的高尔夫球戏，付不了她们音乐间里跳舞用六十几磅的传声机。并不是他舍不得她们花费。不，她们全是顶漂亮，顶好看的女孩子，夏罗也是位了不得的太太，活该她们那么混，真的是，全城里哪一家都比不上他们家那么交际广，体面。可不是，老倪扶先生每回在客厅桌上推着烟匣子让客，听的总是好话，称赞他的太太，称赞他的女孩子，甚至称赞他自己。

　　"你们是个理想的家庭，老先生，一个理想的家庭，仿佛是在书上念剧或是戏台上看的似的。"

　　"算了算了，我的孩子，"老倪扶先生答道，"试试这烟，看合适不合适？你要愿意到花园去抽烟，孩子们大概全在草地上玩着哪。"

所以这群女孩子全没有嫁人，人家就这么说。她们愿意嫁谁都成，可是她们在家太乐了。她们整天地在一起玩，多么乐，女孩子们外加夏罗，哼，哼！得了，得了！许是这么回事……

你已经走完了那条时髦的哈各德大路；他已经到了街角那所屋子，他们的住宅。进出车马的门推在那里；地上有新过的车轮痕迹，他面对着这所白漆的大楼，窗子满开着，花纱的窗帘向外飘着，宽阔的窗沿上摆着玉簪花的蓝瓷花盆。车道的两边满开着他们的紫阳花，全城有名的。一穗粉红的，浅蓝的花，像阳光似的和杂在纷披的叶子中间，老倪扶先生看看屋子，看看花，又看看车道上新印的轮迹，仿佛他们都在对他说此地有的是青年的生活，有的是女孩子们！

外厅里还是老样子，昏沉沉的满是围巾，洋伞，手套等类，全堆在那橡木柜架上。音乐间里有琴声，又快又响，不耐烦的琴声。客厅的门半掩着，漏出里面的人声。

"那么，有冰激凌没有呢？"夏罗的声音，接着她摇椅的轧哩轧哩。

"冰激凌！"安粟叫道，"我的亲娘，你从没有见过那样的冰激凌，就是两种，一种是平常店里的小杨梅水，沿边化得全是水。"

"那饭整个坏得太可怕了。"玛丽安接着说。

"可是，冰激凌总还太早点。"夏罗缓缓地说。

"怎么呢，要有就得好。"安粟又开口。

"对呀！宝贝。"夏罗轻着口音说。

忽然音乐间门"啪"地打开了，老腊冲了进来，他一见老倪扶先生站着，吓了一跳，差一点喊了出来。

"嘎呵，是爹！你吓得我！你才回家吗？怎么的查利士不来帮你脱外套？"

她满脸羞得通红，两眼发光，头发落在额上，她气喘得像方从暗里跑了出来，受了惊似的，原来这就是老腊，是不是，但是她似乎把老子忘了；她等在那里可不是为他；她把持敝了的手绢角放在牙齿中间，恨恨地尽啃着。电话响了，啊啊！老腊"吱"地一声叫，当着他直冲了过去。"嘭"的一声电话间的门关紧了，同时夏罗叫道，"他爹，是你不是？"

"你又乏了。"夏罗抱怨地说着，她停止了她的摇椅，把她暖暖的熟梅似的脸凑上去让他亲吻。

头发烁亮的安粟在他的胡子上啄了一下，玛丽安的口唇刷着他的耳。

"你走回来的，他爹？"夏罗问。

"是，我走回家的。"老倪扶先生说着，在一张客厅大椅里沉了下去。

"可是你为什么不坐个车？"安粟问，"那时候有的是车，要几百都有。"

"我的乖乖安粟，"玛丽安叫道，"要是爹真愿意累坏他自个儿，我看我们也没有法子去干涉。"

"孩子们，孩子们。"夏罗甜着口音劝着。

玛丽安可不肯停嘴。"不，娘，你宠坏了爹，那不对的。你得对他认真点儿，他是顶顽皮。"她笑着，她又硬又响地笑，对着镜子掠她的头发。真怪！她小的时候，嗓子顶软，话也说不出口似的，她有时简直是口吃，可是现在，不论说什么就是在饭桌上的"爹，劳驾梅酱"；她总是唱着高调，仿佛在台上唱戏似的。

"你来的时候海乐尔离了公司没有，我爱？"
夏罗问道，又把坐椅摇了起来。

"我不很清楚。"老倪扶先生说。

"我说不上，四点钟以后我就没有见他。"

"他说……"夏罗正要说下去，安粟在报纸里乱翻了一阵，忽然跑过来，蹲在她娘椅子的旁边叫道："这儿，你看，我说的就是那个。妈，黄的，有点银子的，你不爱吗？"

"给我吧！宝贝。"夏罗说，她摸着了她的玳瑁眼镜，戴上了，把她丰腴的小手指，轻抚着那页纸，把她的口唇荷包似的卷了起来。"哦，真可爱！"她含糊小语着；她从眼镜边儿上面望出来，看看安粟。"我可不喜那裙飘。"

"不喜那裙飘！"安粟哭丧着声音喊道，"好的就是那裙飘。"

"我来，娘让我看。"玛丽安咄地把那页纸从夏罗手中抢了过去。"我说娘对的，"她高兴地喊说，"有了那裙飘，看得太重了。"

老倪扶先生，人家早把他忘了，一和身沉在他坐椅的宽边儿里面，昏昏地假寐着，听她们说话，仿佛在做梦似的。他真是乏了；他再也使不出劲儿。今夜连自己的太太和女孩子们，他都受不住，她们是太……太……

　　他半睡着的在心里所能想着的就只——他是大富了。在什么事情的背后，他都看见有个枯干的小老头儿在爬着无穷尽的楼梯，他是谁呢？

　　"今晚上我不换衣服了。"他含糊地说。"你说什么，爹？""哦！什么，什么。"老倪扶先生惊醒了，睁着眼向她们望。"我今晚上不换衣服了。"他又说一遍。

　　"可是我们请了罗雪儿，达文伯，还有华革太太。"

　　"可这个春天不大好。"

　　"你人好过吗，我爱？"

　　"你自己又不用使劲，要查利士干什么？"

　　"可是你要真是来不得……"夏罗在迟疑。

　　"成，成，成。"老倪扶站了起来，自个儿跑上楼，他方才隐约梦见爬楼梯的那个小老头儿，仿佛就在他面前引路。年轻的查利士已经在更衣房里等他，很小心地他在拿一块手巾围着那热水筒。年轻的查利士，自从脸子红红的小孩子时候到家来收拾火炉以来，就是他得爱的当差。老倪扶先生一进房，坐下在窗口一张藤编的长椅上，伸出了一双腿，照例开他每晚的小玩笑。

"查利士把他打扮起来了！"查利士皱着眉，深深地呼吸着，凑上前去把他领结里的针拔了出来。

哦，哦！好，好！坐在打开的窗前很爽快，很爽快——很温和的黄昏，下面正有人在网球场上剪草；他听得刈草器的咄咄。不久那女孩子们又要开网球会了。一想着球会，他就好像听得玛丽安的声音荡着，"有你的，伙计……打着了，伙计，啊，真好哪！"接着夏罗在廊下叫着，"海乐尔在哪儿？"安粟说，"他总不在这儿，娘。"夏罗又含糊地回着，"他说……"

老倪扶先生叹了一口气，站了起来，一手摸在他胡子的里面，从查利士手里取过梳子，很当心地把他白胡子梳了几道，查利士递给他一块折齐的手帕，他的表和图章，眼镜盒子。"没事了，孩子。"门关上了，他又坐了下去，就是他一个人……

现在那小老头儿又在无穷尽的楼下漂亮的饭厅里，灯火开得旺旺的。

啊！他的腿！像蜘蛛的腿——细小，干瘪了的。

"你们是个理想的家庭。"可是那话要是实，为甚夏罗或是女孩子们不曾留住他。为甚他老是一个人，爬上爬下的，老是一个人。海乐尔在哪里？啊！再不要盼望海乐尔什么事。下去了，那小小的老蜘蛛下去了。老倪扶先生心里害怕，因为他见他溜过了饭厅，出了门，上了暗沉沉的车道，出了车马进出的门，到了公司。你们留住他，留住他，有人没有！

老倪扶先生又惊觉了。他的更衣房里已经黑了，窗口只有些惨淡的光。他睡了有多久？他听着，他听得远远的人声，远远的声浪，穿过这又高又大昏黑了的房子，传到他的耳边。也许，他昏沉地在想，他已经睡得好久了，谁也没有记着他，全忘他，这屋子，夏罗，女孩子们，海乐尔，——与他有什么相干，他知道他们什么事？他们是他的生人。生命已经在他面前过去了。夏罗已不是他的妻子，他的妻子！……黑沉沉的门口，一半让情藤给掩着了，情藤仿佛懂得人情，也在垂头丧气，发愁似的。小的暖的手臂绕着他的项颈。一只又小又白的脸，对他仰着，一个口音说道，"再会罢，我的宝贝。"

"我的宝贝！再会吧，我的宝贝。"她们里面哪一个说的，她们为甚要再会？准是错了，她是他的妻，那个面色苍白的小女孩子，此外他的一生只是一个梦。

这时候门开了，年轻的查利士，站在灯亮里，垂着一双手，像个年轻的兵士，大声喊道，"饭已经端出来了，先生！"

"我来了，我来了！"老倪扶先生说。

# *An Ideal Family*

*T*hat evening for the first time in his life, as he pressed through the swing door and descended the three broad steps to the pavement, old Mr. Neave felt he was too old for the spring. Spring—warm, eager, restless—was there, waiting for him in the golden light, ready in front of everybody to run up, to blow in his white beard, to drag sweetly on his arm. And he couldn't meet her, no; he couldn't square up once more and stride off, jaunty as a young man. He was tired and, although the late sun was still shining, curiously cold, with a numbed feeling all over. Quite suddenly he hadn't the energy, he hadn't the heart to stand this gaiety and bright movement any longer; it confused him. He wanted to stand still, to wave it away with his stick, to say, "Be off with you!" Suddenly it was a terrible effort to greet as usual—tipping his wide-awake with his stick—all the people whom he knew, the friends, acquaintances, shopkeepers, postmen, drivers. But the gay glance that went with the gesture, the kindly twinkle that seemed to say, "I'm a match and more for any of you"—that old Mr. Neave could not manage at all. He stumped along, lifting his knees high as if he were walking through air that had somehow grown heavy and solid like water. And the homeward-looking crowd hurried by, the trams clanked, the light carts clattered, the big swinging cabs bowled along with that reckless, defiant indifference that one knows only in dreams...

It had been a day like other days at the office. Nothing special had happened. Harold hadn't come back from lunch until close on four. Where had he been? What had he been up to? He wasn't going to let his father know. Old Mr. Neave had happened to be in the vestibule, saying good-bye to a caller, when Harold sauntered in, perfectly turned out as usual, cool, suave, smiling that peculiar little half-smile that women found so fascinating.

Ah, Harold was too handsome, too handsome by far; that had been the trouble all along. No man had a right to such eyes, such lashes, and such lips; it was uncanny. As for his mother, his sisters, and the servants, it was not too much to say they made a young god of him; they worshipped Harold, they forgave him everything; and he had needed some forgiving ever since the time when he was thirteen and he had stolen his mother's purse, taken the money, and hidden the purse in the cook's bedroom. Old Mr. Neave struck sharply with his stick upon the pavement edge. But it wasn't only his family who spoiled Harold, he reflected, it was everybody; he had only to look and to smile, and down they went before him. So perhaps it wasn't to be wondered at that he expected the office to carry on the tradition. H'm, h'm! But it couldn't be done. No business—not even a successful, established, big paying concern— could be played with. A man had either to put his whole heart and soul into it, or it went all to pieces before his eyes...

And then Charlotte and the girls were always at him to make the whole thing over to Harold, to retire, and to spend his time enjoying himself. Enjoying himself! Old Mr. Neave stopped dead under a group of ancient cabbage palms outside the Government buildings! Enjoying himself! The wind of evening shook the dark leaves to a thin airy cackle. Sitting at home, twiddling his thumbs, conscious all the while that his life's work was slipping away, dissolving, disappearing through Harold's fine fingers, while Harold smiled...

"Why will you be so unreasonable, father? There's absolutely no need for you to go to the office. It only makes it very awkward for us when people persist in saying how tired you're looking. Here's this huge house and garden. Surely you could be happy in—in—appreciating it for a change. Or you could take up some hobby."

And Lola the baby had chimed in loftily, "All men ought to have hobbies. It makes life impossible if they haven't."

Well, well! He couldn't help a grim smile as painfully he began to climb the hill that led into Harcourt Avenue. Where would Lola and her sisters and Charlotte be if he'd gone in for hobbies, he'd like to know? Hobbies couldn't pay for the town house and the seaside bungalow, and their horses, and their golf, and the sixty-guinea gramophone in the music-room for them to dance to. Not that he grudged them these things. No, they were smart, good-looking girls, and Charlotte was a remarkable woman; it was natural for them to be in the swim. As a matter of fact, no other house in the town was as popular as theirs; no other family entertained so much. And how many times old Mr. Neave, pushing the cigar box across the smoking-room table, had listened to praises of his wife, his girls, of himself even.

"You're an ideal family, sir, an ideal family. It's like something one reads about or sees on the stage."

"That's all right, my boy," old Mr. Neave would

reply. "Try one of those; I think you'll like them. And if you care to smoke in the garden, you'll find the girls on the lawn, I dare say."

That was why the girls had never married, so people said. They could have married anybody. But they had too good a time at home. They were too happy together, the girls and Charlotte. H'm, h'm! Well, well. Perhaps so...

By this time he had walked the length of fashionable Harcourt Avenue; he had reached the corner house, their house. The carriage gates were pushed back; there were fresh marks of wheels on the drive. And then he faced the big white-painted house, with its wide-open windows, its tulle curtains floating outwards, its blue jars of hyacinths on the broad sills. On either side of the carriage porch their hydrangeas—famous in the town—were coming into flower; the pinkish, bluish masses of flower lay like light among the spreading leaves. And somehow, it seemed to old Mr. Neave that the house and the flowers, and even the fresh marks on the drive, were saying, "There is young life here. There are girls—"

The hall, as always, was dusky with wraps, parasols, gloves, piled on the oak chests. From the music-room sounded the piano, quick, loud and impatient. Through the drawing-room door that was ajar voices floated.

"And were there ices?" came from Charlotte. Then the creak, creak of her rocker.

"Ices!" cried Ethel. "My dear mother, you never saw such ices. Only two kinds. And one a common little strawberry shop ice, in a sopping wet frill."

"The food altogether was too appalling," came from Marion.

"Still, it's rather early for ices," said Charlotte easily.

"But why, if one has them at all... "began Ethel.

"Oh, quite so, darling," crooned Charlotte.

Suddenly the music-room door opened and Lola dashed out. She started, she nearly screamed, at the sight of old Mr. Neave.

"Gracious, father! What a fright you gave me!

Have you just come home? Why isn't Charles here to help you off with your coat?"

Her cheeks were crimson from playing, her eyes glittered, the hair fell over her forehead. And she breathed as though she had come running through the dark and was frightened. Old Mr. Neave stared at his youngest daughter; he felt he had never seen her before. So that was Lola, was it? But she seemed to have forgotten her father; it was not for him that she was waiting there. Now she put the tip of her crumpled handkerchief between her teeth and tugged at it angrily. The telephone rang. A-ah! Lola gave a cry like a sob and dashed past him. The door of the telephone-room slammed, and at the same moment Charlotte called, "Is that you, father?"

"You're tired again," said Charlotte reproachfully, and she stopped the rocker and offered her warm plum-like cheek. Bright-haired Ethel pecked his beard, Marion's lips brushed his ear.

"Did you walk back, father?" asked Charlotte.

"Yes, I walked home," said old Mr. Neave, and he

sank into one of the immense drawing-room chairs.

"But why didn't you take a cab?" said Ethel. "There are hundreds of cabs about at that time."

"My dear Ethel," cried Marion, "if father prefers to tire himself out, I really don't see what business of ours it is to interfere."

"Children, children?" coaxed Charlotte.

But Marion wouldn't be stopped. "No, mother, you spoil father, and it's not right. You ought to be stricter with him. He's very naughty." She laughed her hard, bright laugh and patted her hair in a mirror. Strange! When she was a little girl she had such a soft, hesitating voice; she had even stuttered, and now, whatever she said—even if it was only "Jam, please, father"—it rang out as though she were on the stage.

"Did Harold leave the office before you, dear?" asked Charlotte, beginning to rock again.

"I'm not sure," said Old Mr. Neave. "I'm not sure. I didn't see him after four o'clock."

"He said—" began Charlotte.

But at that moment Ethel, who was twitching over the leaves of some paper or other, ran to her mother and sank down beside her chair.

"There, you see," she cried. "That's what I mean, mummy. Yellow, with touches of silver. Don't you agree?"

"Give it to me, love," said Charlotte. She fumbled for her tortoise-shell spectacles and put them on, gave the page a little dab with her plump small fingers, and pursed up her lips. "Very sweet!" she crooned vaguely; she looked at Ethel over her spectacles. "But I shouldn't have the train."

"Not the train!" wailed Ethel tragically. "But the train's the whole point."

"Here, mother, let me decide." Marion snatched the paper playfully from Charlotte. "I agree with mother," she cried triumphantly. "The train overweights it."

Old Mr. Neave, forgotten, sank into the broad lap of his chair, and, dozing, heard them as though he dreamed. There was no doubt about it, he was tired out; he had lost his hold. Even Charlotte and the girls were too much for him to-night. They were too... too... But all his drowsing brain could think of was— too rich for him. And somewhere at the back of everything he was watching a little withered ancient man climbing up endless flights of stairs. Who was he?

"I shan't dress to-night," he muttered.

"What do you say, father?"

"Eh, what, what?" Old Mr. Neave woke with a start and stared across at them. "I shan't dress to-night," he repeated.

"But, father, we've got Lucile coming, and Henry Davenport, and Mrs. Teddie Walker."

"It will look so very out of the picture."

"Don't you feel well, dear?"

"You needn't make any effort. What is Charles for?"

"But if you're really not up to it," Charlotte wavered.

"Very well! Very well!" Old Mr. Neave got up and

went to join that little old climbing fellow just as far as his dressing-room...

There young Charles was waiting for him. Carefully, as though everything depended on it, he was tucking a towel round the hot-water can. Young Charles had been a favourite of his ever since as a little red-faced boy he had come into the house to look after the fires. Old Mr. Neave lowered himself into the cane lounge by the window, stretched out his legs, and made his little evening joke, "Dress him up, Charles!" And Charles, breathing intensely and frowning, bent forward to take the pin out of his tie.

H'm, h'm! Well, well! It was pleasant by the open window, very pleasant—a fine mild evening. They were cutting the grass on the tennis court below; he heard the soft churr of the mower. Soon the girls would begin their tennis parties again. And at the thought he seemed to hear Marion's voice ring out, "Good for you, partner... Oh, played, partner... Oh, very nice indeed." Then Charlotte calling from the veranda, "Where is Harold?" And Ethel, "He's certainly not here, mother." And Charlotte's vague, "He said—"

Old Mr. Neave sighed, got up, and putting one hand under his beard, he took the comb from young Charles, and carefully combed the white beard over. Charles gave him a folded handkerchief, his watch and seals, and spectacle case.

"That will do, my lad." The door shut, he sank back, he was alone...

And now that little ancient fellow was climbing down endless flights that led to a glittering, gay dining-room. What legs he had! They were like a spider's—thin, withered.

"You're an ideal family, sir, an ideal family."

But if that were true, why didn't Charlotte or the girls stop him? Why was he all alone, climbing up and down? Where was Harold? Ah, it was no good expecting anything from Harold. Down, down went the little old spider, and then, to his horror, old Mr. Neave saw him slip past the dining-room and make for the porch, the dark drive, the carriage gates, the office. Stop him, stop him, somebody!

Old Mr. Neave started up. It was dark in his dressing-room; the window shone pale. How long had he been asleep? He listened, and through the big, airy, darkened house there floated far-away voices, far-away sounds. Perhaps, he thought vaguely, he had been asleep for a long time. He'd been forgotten. What had all this to do with him—this house and Charlotte, the girls and Harold—what did he know about them? They were strangers to him. Life had passed him by. Charlotte was not his wife. His wife!

... A dark porch, half hidden by a passion-vine, that drooped sorrowful, mournful, as though it understood. Small, warm arms were round his neck. A face, little and pale, lifted to his, and a voice breathed, "Good-bye, my treasure."

"My treasure! Good-bye, my treasure!" Which of them had spoken? Why had they said good-bye? There had been some terrible mistake. She was his wife, that little pale girl, and all the rest of his life had been a dream.

Then the door opened, and young Charles, standing in the light, put his hands by his side and shouted like a young soldier, "Dinner is on the table, sir!"

"I'm coming, I'm coming," said old Mr. Neave.

# 刮　风

忽然间，怪害怕的，她醒了转来。有什么事？出了什么不了的事似的。不，什么事都没有。就是风，刮着房子，摇着窗，砸响着屋顶上的一块铁皮，连她睡着的床都在直晃。树叶子在窗外乱飞，飞上来，又飞了去。下面马路上飞起一整张的报纸，在半空中直爬，像一只断线鹞，又掉了下去，挂在一株松树上。天冷着哪。夏天完了——这是秋天了——什么都看得寒碜，运货车的铁轮子响着走过，一边一边地摆着；两个中国人肩上扛着安蔬菜筐子的木架子在道上一颠一颠地走着——他们的辫子蓝布衫在风里横着飞。一只白狗跷着一条腿噤着冲过前门。什么都完事了！什么？喔，全完了！她那手指抖抖地编着她的头发，不敢往镜子里看。娘在厅上给祖母说着话。

"蠢死了！这天色还不把晒着的东西全收了

进来……我那块顶精致的小茶桌纱布简直给刮成了破布条儿。那怪味儿是什么呀？麦粥烧焦了。可了不得——这风！"

她十点钟有音乐课。这一想着贝德花芬低半音的调子，就在她的脑子里直转，音波颤动着又长又尖的像是小摇鼓琴儿……史家的曼丽跑到间壁园子里去采菊花省得叫风给白糟蹋了。她的裙子抹上腰身撑开了飞；她想给往下按着，蹲下去把它夹在腿中间，可是不成，呼的它还是往上飞。她身旁的树，草，全摇着。她尽快地采，可是她的心乱着。她也顾不得花，随便乱来——把花连根子都起了出来，胡乱地折着揪着，顿着脚赌咒。

"你们就不会把前门关上的！绕到背后去关。"有人在嚷着。接着她听见宝健："娘，找你说电话。电话，娘。肉铺子的。"

这日子多难过——烦死，真叫人烦。……得，这回她帽子上的宽紧带又炸了。不炸还怎么着。她换上了一顶旧软帽，想走后门溜了出去。可是娘已经见了。

"玛提达，玛提达。快——快快地回来！怎

么着你头上戴的是什么呀？倒像个盖茶壶的软兜子。那一绺长头发又给甩在前面算什么了。"

"我不进来了，娘。我上课去，已经太迟了。"

"赶快回来！"

她不。她不干。她恨娘。"去你的！"她大声叫着，往街上直跑。

海里浪似的，天上云似的，一卷卷大圆股儿的土直迎着来刺人，土里还夹着一点点的稻草，米糠，焙干的肥料。园子里的树大声地叫着，她站着路底那间屋子，普伦先生的家门前，连海的啸响都听着了："啊！……啊！……啊！啊！"但是普伦先生的客厅里还是山洞一样的静。窗子全关着，窗幔拉下一半，她并没来晚。"在她前那女孩子"正练着麦克道威尔的《冰岛歌》。普伦先生转眼过来看着她，半笑不笑的。

"坐下，"他说，"坐那边那个沙发，小姑娘。"

多怪，他那样儿。也不能说他一定怎么笑你……可是总有点儿……这屋子里多清静呀。她喜欢这间屋子。闻着有充毛哔叽，陈烟，菊花的味儿……火炉架上鲁本斯达那相片的背后放着有一大盆那……"送给我的好友洛勃普伦……"那黑色闪光的钢琴上也挂着"孤独"——一个穿白衣服脸上暗沉沉神情悲惨的妇人，坐在一块石头上，她的腿交叠着，她的下巴在她的手上。

"不，不！"普伦先生说，他就靠下身子去，把他的胳膊放在那女孩子的肩膀上，替她弹了一道。这笨劲——她面红了！多可笑！

在她前那女孩子走了；前门"嘭"地关上了。普伦先生回进房来，来回地走着，他那温和的样子，等着她。这事情多怪呀。她的手指儿直发颤，连那音乐书包上的结子都解不下来。这是风刮的……她的心也直跳，仿佛她那裙子准叫风刮得一上一下地乱飞。普伦先生一句话也不说。那张旧的红绒琴凳子够两个人并着坐。普伦先生并着她坐下了。

"我先试试指法好不好？"她问，捧着一双手紧紧地挤。"我也练过一点快指法。"

但是他不回话，竟许他听都没有听见……忽然间他的白净的手带着一个戒指地伸了过来，打开了贝多芬。

"我们稍微来一点大家的吧。"他说。

但是为什么他说话这样的和气——这太和气——倒像他们是老朋友。彼此什么都明白似的。

他慢慢地翻着书篇。她看着他的手——多美的一只手,看得老像是才洗干净似的。

"有了。"普伦先生说。

啊,他那和气的声音——啊,那低半音的调子。这是小鼓声来了……

"我来试一遍好不好?"

"好,好孩子。"

他的声音是太,太过分地和气了。那乐谱上的半音符与快半音符直跳着,像是一群黑小孩子在墙篱上跳着玩似的。他为什么这……她不哭——她没有什么要哭的……

"怎么了,好孩子?"

普伦先生拿了她的手,他的肩膀正挨着她的头。她就这一点点儿靠着他的肩,她的脸挨着那疏松的花呢。

"做人没有意思。"她低声地说,可是她一点也不觉得没有意思。他也说了些什么"等一等",

"小心拍板"，"那珍贵的东西，一个女人"，但是她没有听着。这多舒服……老是这……

　　突然间门开了，史家的曼丽蹿了进来，离她的时候还远着远着哪。

　　"这快调还得快一点。"普伦先生说，他站了起来，又在屋子里来回地走着。

　　"坐那沙发椅，小姑娘。"他对曼丽说。

　　这风，这风。一个人坐在她自个儿屋子里怪害怕的。那床，那镜子，那脸盆小壶，全亮着，像外面的天。这张床就叫人怕。它躺在那里，睡得着着的……娘得知不得知这被盖上放着一纠纠像蛇盘似的袜子全得我补？她再不想。不，娘。我不知道为什么，我一定得……这风，这风！烟囱里刮下来有煤灰味儿。有谁写诗给风的？……"我带花给叶子给雨"……胡扯。

　　"是你呀，宝健？"

　　"来同我到海边上去走走，玛提达。这我再也受不住了。"

　　"有理，让我披上外套。这天多坏！"宝健的外套跟她的一样。扣上了领子她对镜子里照了照自己。她脸是白的，他们俩一样有那火亮的眼，

火热的嘴。啊，镜子里的一对他们认识。再见，
乖乖；我们就回来的。

"这样好，是不是？"

"扣上了。"宝健说。

他们走得总不够快。低着头，腿正碰着，他
们俩看是一个急忙忙的人，走完大街，走下那不
整齐的沥青道满长着小茴香花的，这下去就是靠
海那块平地。天晚了——正是黄昏时。大风刮得
她们俩走都走不稳，冲着风左颠右跛地像一对酒
醉鬼。大场上的野草花儿全叫风给吹倒了。

"来呀！来呀！我们走近一点。"

过了那堤防，外面的海里浪起得顶高。她们
脱了帽子，她的头发腌在她的嘴里，满是盐味
儿，海里风太大了，浪头直往上鼓，也不开花；
浪上来嗤嗤地打着堤防的大石壁，长草的滴水的
石级全叫淹了去。一股劲浪直冲了过来。她们身
上全是水点；她的嘴里尝着又湿又凉的。

宝健说着话哪，他说话声音一高一低的，顶
怪的——听了可笑——可是那天正合适。风带着
他们的声音———一句句话直往外飞像是一条条小
的窄的丝带。

"快一点！快一点！"

天愈迟愈黑了。海湾里上煤的靠船上有两个亮——一个高高的在桅上，一个在船梢上。

"看，宝健。看那边。"

一只大的黑轮船冒着一大卷烟，船舱圆窗洞里全默着亮，船上那处全是亮，正在开出去。大风留不住它；它破着浪走，向着那两边是光石子的湾门口去，这去是到……就这光过来显得它异样，又美又神秘的……他们俩臂挽臂地在船栏上靠着哪。

"……他们是谁？"

"弟弟跟姊。"

"看，宝健，那是我们的镇。看得真小不是？那是最末了一次的邮局钟。那是那块大场地，那天大风天我们在走着的。你记得不？那天我上音乐课还哭哪——多少年前的事！再会吧，小岛，再会……"

这忽见黑夜伸出一个翅膀盖住了沸翻的海水。他们瞧不见他们俩了。再会，再会。别忘了……但是那船已经走了！这时候。

## *The Wind Blows*

Suddenly—dreadfully—she wakes up. What has happened? Something dreadful has happened. No—nothing has happened. It is only the wind shaking the house, rattling the windows, banging a piece of iron on the roof and making her bed tremble. Leaves flutter past the window, up and away; down in the avenue a whole newspaper wags in the air like a lost kite and falls, spiked on a pine tree. It is cold. Summer is over—it is autumn—everything is ugly. The carts rattle by, swinging from side to side; two Chinamen lollop along under their wooden yokes with the straining vegetable baskets—their pigtails and blue blouses fly out in the wind. A white dog on three legs yelps past the gate. It is all over! What is? Oh, everything! And she begins to plait her hair with shaking fingers, not daring to look in the glass. Mother is talking to grandmother in the hall.

"A perfect idiot! Imagine leaving anything out on the line in weather like this... Now my best little Teneriffe-work teacloth is simply in ribbons. What is that extraordinary smell? It's the porridge burning. Oh, heavens—this wind!"

She has a music lesson at ten o'clock. At the thought the minor movement of the Beethoven begins to play in her head, the trills long and terrible like little rolling drums... Marie Swainson runs into the garden next door to pick the "chrysanths" before they are ruined. Her skirt flies up above her waist; she tries to beat it down, to tuck it between her legs while she stoops, but it is no use—up it flies. All the trees and bushes beat about her. She picks as quickly as she can but she is quite distracted. She doesn't mind what she does—she pulls the plants up by the roots and bends and twists them, stamping her foot and swearing.

"For heaven's sake keep the front door shut! Go

round to the back," shouts someone. And then she hears Bogey,

"Mother, you're wanted on the telephone. Telephone, Mother. It's the butcher."

How hideous life is—revolting, simply revolting... And now her hat-elastic's snapped. Of course it would. She'll wear her old tam and slip out the back way. But Mother has seen.

"Matilda. Matilda. Come back im-me-diately! What on earth have you got on your head? It looks like a tea cosy. And why have you got that mane of hair on your forehead."

"I can't come back. Mother. I'll be late for my lesson."

"Come back immediately!"

She won't. She won't. She hates Mother. "Go to hell," she shouts, running down the road.

In waves, in clouds, in big round whirls the dust comes stinging, and with it little bits of straw and chaff and manure. There is a loud roaring sound from the trees in the gardens, and standing at the bottom of the road outside Mr. Bullen's gate she can hear the sea sob, "Ah! ... Ah! ... Ah-h!" But Mr. Bullen's drawing-room is as quiet as a cave. The windows are closed, the blinds half pulled, and she is not late. The-girl-before-her has just started playing MacDowell's "To an Iceberg". Mr. Bullen looks over at her and half smiles.

"Sit down," he says. "Sit over there in the sofa corner, little lady."

How funny he is. He doesn't exactly laugh at you... but there is just something... Oh, how peaceful it is here. She likes this room. It smells of art serge and stale smoke and chrysanthemums... there is a big vase of them on the mantelpiece behind the pale photograph of Rubinstein... à mon ami Robert Bullen... Over the black glittering piano hangs "Solitude"—a dark tragic woman draped in white, sitting on a rock, her knees crossed, her chin on her hands.

"No, no!" says Mr. Bullen, and he leans over the other girl, put his arms over her shoulders and plays

the passage for her. The stupid—she's blushing!
How ridiculous!

Now the-girl-before-her has gone; the front
door slams. Mr. Bullen comes back and walks up
and down, very softly, waiting for her. What an
extraordinary thing. Her fingers tremble so that she
can't undo the knot in the music satchel. It's the
wind... And her heart beats so hard she feels it must
lift her blouse up and down. Mr. Bullen does not say
a word. The shabby red piano seat is long enough for
two people to sit side by side. Mr. Bullen sits down
by her.

"Shall I begin with scales," she asks, squeezing
her hands together. "I had some arpeggios, too."

But he does not answer. She doesn't believe he
even hears... and then suddenly his fresh hand with
the ring on it reaches over and opens Beethoven.

"Let's have a little of the old master," he says.

But why does he speak so kindly—so awfully
kindly—and as though they had known each other
for years and years and knew everything about each

other.

He turns the page slowly. She watches his hand—it is a very nice hand and always looks as though it had just been washed.

"Here we are," says Mr. Bullen.

Oh, that kind voice—Oh, that minor movement. Here come the little drums...

"Shall I take the repeat?"

"Yes, dear child."

His voice is far, far too kind. The crotchets and quavers are dancing up and down the stave like little black boys on a fence. Why is he so... She will not cry—she has nothing to cry about...

"What is it, dear child?"

Mr. Bullen takes her hands. His shoulder is there—just by her head. She leans on it ever so little, her cheek against the springy tweed.

"Life is so dreadful," she murmurs, but she does not feel it's dreadful at all. He says something about "waiting" and "marking time" and "that rare thing, a woman", but she does not hear. It is so comfortable...

for ever...

Suddenly the door opens and in pops Marie Swainson, hours before her time.

"Take the allegretto a little faster," says Mr. Bullen, and gets up and begins to walk up and down again.

"Sit in the sofa corner, little lady," he says to Marie.

The wind, the wind. It's frightening to be here in her room by herself. The bed, the mirror, the white jug and basin gleam like the sky outside. It's the bed that is frightening. There it lies, sound asleep... Does Mother imagine for one moment that she is going to darn all those stockings knotted up on the quilt like a coil of snakes? She's not. No, Mother. I do not see why I should... The wind—the wind! There's a funny smell of soot blowing down the chimney. Hasn't anyone written poems to the wind?... "I bring fresh flowers to the leaves and showers."... What nonsense.

"Is that you, Bogey?"

"Come for a walk round the esplanade, Matilda. I can't stand this any longer."

"Right-o. I'll put on my ulster. Isn't it an awful day!" Bogey's ulster is just like hers. Hooking the collar she looks at herself in the glass. Her face is white, they have the same excited eyes and hot lips. Ah, they know those two in the glass. Good-bye, dears; we shall be back soon.

"This is better, isn't it?"

"Hook on," says Bogey.

They cannot walk fast enough. Their heads bent, their legs just touching, they stride like one eager person through the town, down the asphalt zigzag where the fennel grows wild and on to the esplanade. It is dusky—just getting dusky. The wind is so strong that they have to fight their way through it, rocking like two old drunkards. All the poor little pahutukawas on the esplanade are bent to the ground.

"Come on! Come on! Let's get near."

Over by the breakwater the sea is very high.

They pull off their hats and her hair blows across her mouth, tasting of salt. The sea is so high that the waves do not break at all; they thump against the rough stone wall and suck up the weedy, dripping steps. A fine spray skims from the water right across the esplanade. They are covered with drops; the inside of her mouth tastes wet and cold.

Bogey's voice is breaking. When he speaks he rushes up and down the scale. It's funny—it makes you laugh—and yet it just suits the day. The wind carries their voices—away fly the sentences like little narrow ribbons.

"Quicker! Quicker!"

It is getting very dark. In the harbour the coal hulks show two lights—one high on a mast, and one from the stern.

"Look, Bogey. Look over there."

A big black steamer with a long loop of smoke streaming, with the portholes lighted, with lights everywhere, is putting out to sea. The wind does not stop her; she cuts through the waves, making for the

open gate between the pointed rocks that leads to...
It's the light that makes her look so awfully beautiful
and mysterious... They are on board leaning over the
rail arm in arm.

"... Who are they?"

"... Brother and sister."

"Look, Bogey, there's the town. Doesn't it look
small? There's the post office clock chiming for the
last time. There's the esplanade where we walked
that windy day. Do you remember? I cried at my
music lesson that day—how many years ago! Good-
bye, little island, good-bye..."

Now the dark stretches a wing over the tumbling
water. They can't see those two any more. Good-bye,
good-bye. Don't forget... But the ship is gone, now.

The wind—the wind.

# 曼殊斐尔

徐志摩

这心灵深处的欢畅，

这情绪境界的壮旷：

任天堂沉沦，地狱开放，

毁不了我内府的宝藏！

——徐志摩《康河晚照即景》

美感的记忆，是人生最可珍的产业。认识美的本能，是上帝给我们进天堂的一把秘钥。

有人的性情，例如我自己的，如以气候作喻，不但是阴晴相间，而且常有狂风暴雨，也有最艳丽蓬勃的春光。有时遭逢幻灭，引起厌世的悲观，铅般地重压在心上，比如冬令阴霾，到处冰结，莫有些微生气；那时便怀疑一切：宇宙，人生，自我，都只是幻的妄的；人情，希望，理想，也只是妄的幻的。


      Ah，human nature，how，

      If utterly frail thou art and vile，

      If dust thou art and ashes，is thy heart so great？

      If thou art noble in part，

      How are thy loftiest and impulses and thoughts

      By so ignoble causes kindled and put out？

      "Sopra un ritratto di una bella donna" [1]


　　这几行是最深入的悲观派诗人理巴第（Leopardi）的诗；一座荒坟的墓碑上，刻着冢中人生前美丽的肖像，激起了他这根本的疑问——若说人生是有理可寻的，何以到处只是矛盾的现

---

　　① 啊，人性，是怎样呢/若全然脆弱或卑贱至极，/若是尘埃与灰烬，/你的心怎又这般伟大？/若你还有些高贵，/那你最高贵的冲动和想法/怎这般微不足道地燃起又熄灭？

　　最后一句是意大利文诗句的一节，原句意为："在美人的墓碑上刻着她的美丽肖像。"

象，若说美是幻的，何以引起的心灵反动能有如此之深刻；若说美是真的，何以也与常物同归腐朽？但理巴第探海灯似的智力虽则把人间种种事物虚幻的外象，一一给褫剥了，连宗教都剥成了个赤裸的梦，他却没有力量来否认美，美的创现他只能认为是神奇的；他也不能否认高洁的精神恋，虽则他不信女子也能有同样的境界。在感美感恋最纯粹的一刹那，理巴第不能不承认是极乐天国的消息，不能不承认是生命中最宝贵的经验。所以我每次无聊到极点的时候，在层冰般严封的心河底里，突然涌起一股消融一切的热流，顷刻间消融了厌世的凝晶，消融了烦恼的苦冻：那热流便是感美感恋最纯粹的一俄顷之回忆。

To see a world in a grain of sand,

And a Heaven in a wild flower,

Hold infinity in the palm of your hand,

And eternity in an hour…

(*Auguries of Innocence*：William Blake.)

从一颗沙里看出世界，

天堂的消息在一朵野花，

将无限存在你的掌上，

刹那间涵有无穷的边涯……

（《天真的预言》：威廉·布莱克。）

这类神秘性的感觉，当然不是普遍的经验，也不是常有的经验。凡事只讲实际的人，当然嘲讽神秘主义，当然不能相信科学可解释的神经作用，会发生科学所不能解释的神秘感觉。但世上"可为知者道不可与不知者言"的事正多着哩！

从前在十六世纪，有一次有一个意大利的牧师学者到英国乡下去，见了一大片盛开的苜蓿在阳光中竟同一湖欢舞的黄金，他只惊喜得手足无措，慌忙跪在地上，仰天祷告，感谢上帝的恩典，使他见得这样的美，这样的神景。他这样发疯似的举动，当时一定招起在旁乡下人的哗笑。我这篇要讲的经历，恐怕也有些那牧师狂喜的疯态，但我也深信读者里自有同情的人，所以我也不怕遭乡下人的笑话！

去年七月中有一天晚上，天雨地湿，我独自冒着雨在伦敦的海姆司堆特（Hampstead）问路

警，问行人，在寻彭德街第十号的屋子。那就是
我初次，不幸也是末次，会见曼殊斐尔——"那
二十分不死的时间！"——的一晚。

我先认识麦雷君（John Middleton Murry），
他是 *Atheneaum*[①] 的总主笔，诗人，著名评论家，
也是曼殊斐尔一生最后十余年间最密切的伴侣。

他和她自一九一三年起，即夫妇相处，
但曼殊斐尔却始终用她到英国以后的"笔
名"Katharine Mansfield，她生长于纽新兰（New
Zealand），原名是 Kathleen Beanchamp，是纽新
兰银行经理 Sir Harold Beanchamp 的女儿。她
十五年前离开了本乡，同着三个小妹子到英国，
进伦敦大学皇后学院读书。她从小就以美慧著
名，但身体也从小即很怯弱。她曾在德国住过，
那时她写她的第一本小说 *In a German Pension*[②]。
大战期内她在法国的时候多。近几年她也常在瑞
典意大利及法国南部。她常住外国，就为她身体
太弱，禁不得英伦雾迷雨苦的天时，麦雷为了伴

---

① 《雅典娜神殿》杂志，英国十九世纪的文艺
刊物。
② 《在德国公寓里》。

她，也只得把一部分的事业放弃（*Atheneaum* 之所以并入 *London Nation*① 就为此）。跟着他安琪儿似的爱妻，寻求健康。据说可怜的曼殊斐尔战后得了肺病，证明以后，医生明说她不过两三年的寿限，所以麦雷和她相处有限的光阴，真是分秒可数。多见一次夕照，多经一次朝旭，她优昙似的余荣，便也消减了如许的活力，这颇使人想起茶花女一面吐血一面纵酒恣欢时的名句：

"You know I have not long to live，Therefore I will live fast！"——你知道我是活不久长的，所以我存心活他一个痛快！

我正不知道多情的麦雷，眼看这艳丽无双的夕阳，渐渐消翳，心里"爱莫能助"的悲感，浓烈到何等田地！

但曼殊斐尔的"活他一个痛快"的方法，却不是像茶花女的纵酒恣欢，而是在文艺中努力；她像夏夜榆林中的鹃鸟，呕出缕缕的心血来制成无双的情曲，便唱到血枯音嘶，也还不忘她的责任是牺牲自己有限的精力，替自然界多增几分的

---

① 伦敦的《国民》杂志。

美，给苦闷的人间几分艺术化精神的安慰。

她心血所凝成的便是两本小说集，一本是
*Bliss*①，一本是去年出版的 *Garden Party*②。凭这两
部书里的二三十篇小说，她已经在英国的文学界
里占了一个很稳固的位置。一般的小说只是小
说，她的小说是纯粹的文学，真的艺术；平常的
作者只求暂时的流行，博群众的欢迎，她却只想
留下几小块"时灰"掩不暗的真晶，只要得少数
知音者的赞赏。

但唯其是纯粹的文学，她的著作的光彩是深
蕴于内而不是显露于外的，其趣味也须读者用心
咀嚼，方能充分地理会。我承作者当面许可选译
她的精品，如今她去世，我更应当珍重实行我翻
译的特权，虽则我颇怀疑我自己的胜任。我的好
友陈通伯他所知道的欧州文学恐怕在北京比谁都
更渊博些，他在北大教短篇小说，曾经讲过曼殊
斐尔的，这很使我欢喜。他现在也答应来选译几
篇，我更要感谢他了。关于她短篇艺术的长处，
我也希望通伯能有机会说一点。

①《幸福》。
②《园会》。

现在让我讲那晚怎样地会晤曼殊斐尔。早几天我和麦雷在 Charing Cross① 背后一家嘈杂的 A.B.C. 茶店里，讨论英法文坛的状况，我乘便说起近几年中国文艺复兴的趋向，在小说里感受俄国作者的影响最深，他喜得几乎跳了起来，因为他们夫妻最崇拜俄国的几位大家，他曾经特别研究过陀思妥耶夫斯基，著有一本 Dostoievsky: A Critical Study②，曼殊斐尔又是私淑契诃甫（Chekhov）③ 的，他们常在抱憾俄国文学始终不曾受英国人相当的注意，因之小说的质与式，还脱不尽维多利亚时期的 Philistinism④。我又乘便问起曼殊斐尔的近况，他说她一时身体颇过得去，所以此次敢伴着她回伦敦住两星期，他就给了我他们的住址，请我星期四晚上去会她和他们的朋友。

所以我会见曼殊斐尔，真算是凑巧的凑巧。星期三那天我到惠尔斯（H.G.Wells）乡里的家

① 查令十字街。伦敦书店聚集的街区。
② 《陀思妥耶夫斯基：批评的研究》。
③ 通译契诃夫。
④ 庸俗主义。

去了（Easten Glebe），下一天和他的夫人一同回伦敦，那天雨下得很大，我记得回寓时浑身全淋湿了。

　　他们在彭德街的寓处，很不容易找（伦敦寻地方总是麻烦的，我恨极了那回街曲巷的伦敦），后来居然寻着了，一家小小一楼一底的屋子，麦雷出来替我开门，我颇狼狈地拿着雨伞，还拿着一个朋友还我的几卷中国字画。进了门，我脱了雨具，他让我进右首一间屋子，我到那时为止对于曼殊斐尔只是对于一个有名的年轻女子作者的景仰与期望；至于她的"仙姿灵态"我那时绝对没有想到，我以为她只是与 Rose Macaulay，Virginia Woolf，Roma Wilon，Venessa Bell 几位女文学家的同流人物。平常男子文学家与美术家，已经尽够怪僻，近代女子文学家更似乎故意养成怪僻的习惯，最显著的一个通习是装饰之务淡朴，务不入时，务"背女性"；头发是剪了的，又不好好地收拾，一团糟地散在肩上；袜子永远是粗纱的；鞋上不是沾有泥就是带灰，并且大都是最难看的样式；裙子不是异样地短就是过分地长；眉目间也许有一两圈"天才的黄晕",或是带着最可厌的美国式龟壳大眼镜,但她们的脸上却从不见脂粉的痕迹,手上装饰亦是永远没有的,至多无非是多烧了香烟的焦痕;哗笑的声音,十次有九次半盖过同座的男子;走起路来也是挺胸凸肚的,再也辨不出是夏娃的后身;开起口来大半是男子不敢出口的话;当然最喜欢讨论是 Freudian Complex[1],Birth Control[2],或是 George Moore 与 James Joyce[3] 私人印行的新书,例如 *A Storytellers Holiday* 与 *Ulysses*[4]。总之她们的全人格只是一幅妇女解放的讽刺画(Amy Lowell 听说整天的抽大雪茄)。和这一班立意反对上帝造人的本意的"唯智的"女子在一起,当然也有许多有趣味的地方,但有时总不免感觉她们矫揉造作的痕迹过深,引起一种性的憎忌。

我当时未见曼殊斐尔以前,固然没有想她是这样一流的 Futuristic[5],但也绝对没有梦想到她是女性的理想化。

---

① 弗洛伊德情结。
② 生育控制。
③ 爱尔兰作家乔治·摩尔和乔伊斯。
④ 《一个小说家的假日》与《尤利西斯》。
⑤ 未来主义的。

　　所以我推进那门时我就盼望她——一个将近中年和蔼的妇人——笑盈盈地从壁炉前沙发上站起来和我握手问安。

　　但房里——一间狭长的壁炉对门的房——只见鹅黄色恬静的灯光，壁上炉架上杂色的美术的陈设和画件，几张有彩色画套的沙发围列在炉前，却没有一半个人影。麦雷让我一张椅上坐了，伴着我谈天，谈的是东方的观音和耶教的圣母，希腊的 Virgin Diana① 埃及的 Isis② 波斯 Mithraism③ 里的 Virgin④ 等等之相仿佛，似乎处女的圣母是所有宗教里一个不可少的象征……我们正讲着，只听门上一声剥啄，接着进来了一位年轻的女郎，含笑着站在门口。"难道她就是曼殊斐尔——这样的年轻……"我心里在疑惑，她一头的褐色卷发，盖着一张小圆脸，眼极活泼，口也很灵动，配着一身极鲜艳的衣装——漆鞋，绿

① 狄安娜，神话中代表纯洁的月亮和狩猎女神。
② 伊希斯，古代埃及生育和繁殖女神。
③ 密特拉教。密特拉原为波斯神灵，后传入罗马形成密特拉教。
④ 圣处女。此处或为波斯神话中掌管生育的女神阿娜希塔。

丝长袜，银红绸的上衣，酱紫的丝绒裙——亭亭
地立着，像一颗临风的郁金香。

　　麦雷起来替我介绍，我才知道她不是曼殊斐
尔，而是屋主人，不知是密斯 B——什么，我记
不清了，麦雷是暂寓在她家的；她是个画家，壁
上挂的画，大都是她自己的作品。她在我对面的
椅子上坐了。她从炉架上取下一个小发电机似的
东西拿在手里，头上又戴了一个接电话生戴的听
簹，向我凑得很近地说话，我先还当是无线电的
玩具，随后方知这位秀美的女郎的听觉是有缺
陷的！

　　她正坐定，外面的门铃大响——我疑心她的
门铃是特别响些。来的是我在法兰先生（Roger
Fry）家里会过的 Sydney Waterloo，极诙谐的
一位先生，有一次他从巨大的口袋里一连掏出
了七八支的烟斗，大的小的长的短的，各种颜
色的，叫我们好笑。他进来就问麦雷，迦赛林
（Kathleen，曼殊斐尔原名）今天怎样，我竖了耳
朵听他的回答。麦雷说："她今天不下楼了，天
气太坏，谁都不受用……"华德鲁先生就问他可
否上楼去看她，麦说可以的。华又问了密斯 B 的

允许站了起来，他正要走出门，麦雷又赶过去轻
轻地说"Sydney，don't talk too much"。

　　楼上微微听得出步响，W 已在迦赛林房中
了。一面又来了两个客，一个短的 M 才从游希
腊回来，一个轩昂的美丈夫，就是 *London Nation
and Atheneaum* 里 每 周 做 科 学 文 章 署 名 S 的
Sullivan。M 就讲他游历希腊的情形，尽背着古
希腊的史迹名胜，Parnassus[①] 长，Mycenae[②] 短，
讲个不住。S 也问麦雷迦赛林如何，麦雷说今晚
不下楼，W 现在楼上。过了半点钟模样，W 笨
重的足音下来了，S 问他迦赛林倦了没有，W 说：
"不，不像倦，可是我也说不上，我怕她累，所
以我下来了。"再等一歇，S 也问了麦雷的允许
上楼去，麦也照样叮咛他不要让她乏了。麦问我
中国的书画，我乘便就拿那晚带去的一幅赵之谦
的《草书法画梅》，一幅王觉斯的草书，一幅梁
山舟的行书，打开给他们看，讲了些书法大意，

---

　　① 帕纳塞斯山，希腊地名，古时被当做太阳神和文
艺女神们的灵地。
　　② 迈锡尼，希腊南部城市，希腊大陆青铜晚期文化
的主要遗址。

密斯 B 听得高兴，手捧着她的听盘，挨近我身旁坐着。

但我那时心里却颇觉失望，因为冒着雨存心要来一会 *Bliss* 的作者，偏偏她不下楼，同时 W、S、麦雷的烘云托月，又增了我对她的好奇心。我想运气不好，迦赛林在楼上，老朋友还有进房去谈的特权，我外国人的生客，一定是没有份的了。时已十时过半了，我只得起身告别，走出房门，麦雷陪出来帮我穿雨衣。我一面穿衣，一面说我很抱歉，今晚密斯曼殊斐尔不能下来，否则我是很想望会她一面的，不意麦雷竟很诚恳地说："如其你不介意，不妨请上楼去一见。"我听了这话喜出望外，立即将雨衣脱下，跟着麦雷一步一步地走上楼梯……

上了楼梯，叩门，进房，介绍，S 告辞，和 M 一同出房，关门，她请我坐下，我坐下，她也坐下……这么一大串繁复的手续我只觉得是像电火似的一抹过，其实我只推想应有这么些的经过，却并不曾觉到：当时只觉得一阵模糊。事后每次回想也只觉得是一阵模糊，我们平常从黑暗的街上走进一间灯烛辉煌的屋子，或是从光薄的屋子里出来骤然对着盛烈的阳光，往往觉得耀光太强，头晕目眩的，得定一定神，方能辨认眼前的事物。用英文说就是 Senses overwhelmed by excessive light[1]；不仅是光，浓烈的颜色有时也有"潮没"官觉的效能。我想我那时，虽不定是被曼殊斐尔人格的烈光所潮没，她房里的灯光陈设以及她自身衣饰种种各品浓艳灿烂的颜色，已够使我不预防的神经，感觉刹那间的淆惑，那是很可理解的。

　　她的房给我的印象并不清切，因为她和我谈话时，不容我去认记房中的布置，我只知道房是很小，一张大床差不多就占了全房大部分的地位，壁是用画纸裱的，挂着好几幅油画大概也是主人画的。她和我同坐在床左贴壁一张沙发榻上，因为我斜倚她正坐的缘故，她似乎比我高得多。（在她面前哪一个不是低的，真是！）我疑心那两盏电灯是用红色罩的，否则何以我想起那房，便联想起"红烛高烧"的景象？但背景究属不甚重要，重要的是给我最纯粹的美感的——

---

　　① 强光将直觉淹没。

The pure of aesthetic feeling——她，是使我使用上帝给我那把进天国的秘钥的——她，是使我灵魂的内府里，又增加了一部宝藏的——她。但要用不驯服的文字来描写那晚的她！不要说显示她人格的精华，就是单只忠实地表现我当时的单纯感象，恐怕就够难的了。从前一个人有一次做梦，进天堂去玩了，他异样地欢喜，明天一起身就到他朋友那里去，想描写他神妙不过的梦境，但是！他站在朋友面前，结住舌头，一个字都说不出来，因为他要说的时候，才觉得他所学的在人间适用的字句，绝对不能表现他梦里所见天堂的景色，他气得从此不开口，后来抑郁而死。我此时妄想用字来活现出一个曼殊斐尔，也差不多有同样的感觉，但我却宁可冒猥渎神灵的罪，免得像那位诚实君子活活地闷死。她的打扮与她的朋友 B 女士相像：也是烁亮的漆皮鞋，闪色的绿丝袜，枣红丝绒的围裙，嫩黄薄绸的上衣，领口是尖开的，胸前挂着一串细珍珠，袖口只齐及肘弯。她的发是黑的，也同密斯 B 一样剪短的，但她栉发的样式，却是我在欧美从没有见过的。我疑心她是有心仿效中国式，因为她的发不但纯黑，而且直而不鬈，整整齐齐的一圈，前面像我们十余年前的"刘海"，梳得光滑异常；我虽则说不出所以然，但觉得她发之美也是生平所仅见。

至于她眉目口鼻之清之秀之明净，我其实不能传神于万一；仿佛你对着自然界的杰作，不论是秋水洗净的湖山，霞彩纷披的夕照，或是南洋莹彻的星空，或是艺术界的杰作，培德花芬[1]的沁芳[2]，南怀格纳[3]的奥佩拉[4]，密克郎其罗[5]的雕像，卫师德拉（Whistler）[6]或是柯罗（Corot）的画；你只觉得他们整体的美，纯粹的美，完全的美，不能分析的美，可感不可说的美；你仿佛直接无碍地领会了造化最高明的意志，你在最伟大深刻的戟刺中经验了无限的欢喜，在更大的人格中解化了你的性灵。我看了曼殊斐尔像印度最纯澈的碧玉似的容貌，受着她充满了灵魂的电流的

---

[1] 通译贝多芬。
[2] 交响乐symphony的音译。
[3] 通译瓦格纳。
[4] 歌剧opera的音译。
[5] 通译米开朗基罗。
[6] 通译惠斯勒。

凝视，感着她最和软的春风似的神态，所得的总量我只能称之为一整个的美感。她仿佛是个透明体，你只感讶她粹极的灵彻性，却看不见一些杂质。就是她一身的艳服，如其别人穿着，也许会引起琐碎的批评，但在她身上，你只是觉得妥帖，像牡丹的绿叶，只是不可少的衬托，汤林生（H.M.Tomlingson 她生前的一个好友），以阿尔帕斯山岭万古不融的雪，来比拟她清极超俗的美，我以为很有意味的。他说——

　　曼殊斐尔以美称，然美固未足以状其真，世以可人为美，曼殊斐尔固可人矣，然何其脱尽尘寰气，一若高山琼雪，清彻重霄，其美可惊，而其凉亦可感。艳阳被雪，幻成异彩，亦明明可识，然亦似神境在远，不隶人间。曼殊斐尔肌肤明皙如纯牙，其官之秀，其目之黑，其颊之腴，其约发环整如鬃，其神态之娴静，有华族粲者之明粹，而无西艳伉杰之容；其躯体尤苗约，绰如也，若明蜡之静焰，若晨星之澹妙，就语者未尝不自讶其吐息之重浊，而虑是静且澹者之且神化……

汤林生又说她锐敏的目光，似乎直接透入你的灵府深处，将你所蕴藏的秘密，一齐照彻，所以他说她有鬼气，有仙气；她对着你看，不是见你的面之表，而是见你心之底，但她却不是侦刺你的内蕴，不是有目的地搜罗，而只是同情地体贴。你在她面前，自然会感觉对她无慎密的必要；你不说她也有数，你说了她不会惊讶。她不会责备，她不会怂恿，她不会奖赞，她不会代你出什么物质利益的主意，她只是默默地听，听完了然后对你讲她自己超于善恶的见解——真理。

这一段从长期的交谊中出来深入的话，我与她仅仅一二十分钟的接近当然不会体会到，但我敢说从她神灵的目光里推测起来，这几句话不但是可能，而且是极近情的。

所以我那晚和她同坐在蓝丝绒的榻上，幽静的灯光，轻笼住她美妙的全体，我像受了催眠似的，只是痴对她神灵的妙眼，一任她利剑似的光波，妙乐似的音浪，狂潮骤雨似的向我灵府泼淹。我那时即使有自觉的感觉，也只似开茨

（Keats）① 听鹃啼时的：


> My heart aches, and a drowsy
>
>   numbness pains
>
> My sense, as though of homleck I had drunk…
>
> Tis not through envy of thy happy lot
>
> But being too happy in thy happiness…


　　曼殊斐尔的声音之美，又是一个miracle②。一个个音符从她脆弱的声带里颤动出来，都在我习于尘俗的耳中，启示着一种神奇的意境，仿佛蔚蓝的天空中一颗一颗的明星先后涌现。像听音乐似的，虽则明明你一生从不曾听过，但你总觉得好像曾经闻到过的，也许在梦里，也许在前生。她的，不仅引起你听觉的美感，而竟似直达你的心灵底里，抚摩你蕴而不宣的苦痛，温和你半冷半僵的希望，洗涤你窒碍性灵的俗累，增加你精神快乐的情调，仿佛凑住你灵魂的耳畔私语你平日所冥想不到的仙界消息。我便此时回想，还不

---

① 通译济慈。
② 奇迹。

禁内动感激的悲慨，几乎零泪；她是去了，她的
音声笑貌也似霞彩似的一霎不再，我只能学 Abt
Vogler 之自慰，虔信——


> Whose voice has gone forth,
> But each survives for the melodies when
> 　　eternity affirms the conception of an hour.
> ……
> Enough that he heard it once,
> We shall hear it by and by.[①]


　　曼殊斐尔，我前面说过，是病肺痨的，我见
她时正离她死不过半年，她那晚说话时，声音稍
高，肺管中便如获管似的呼呼作响，她每句语尾
收顿时，总有些气促，颧颊间便也多添一层红
润，我当时听出了她肺弱的音息，便觉得切心的
难过，而同时她天才的兴奋，偏是逼迫她音度的
提高，音愈高，肺嘶亦更呖呖，胸间的起伏，亦
隐约可辨，可怜！我无奈何，只得将自己的声音

---

　　① 声音已然传去，/但每段旋律都在此留存，当一小时
成为永恒。……/他听过一次足矣，/我们终究也会听闻。

特别地放低，希冀她也跟着放低些。果然很应效，她也放低了不少，但不久她又似内感思想的载刺，重复节节地高引。最后我再也不忍因我而多耗她珍贵的精力，并且也记得麦雷再三叮嘱 W 与 S 的话，就辞了出来，总计我进房至出房——她站在房口送我——不过二十分的时间。

　　我与她所讲的话也很有意味，但大部分是她对于英国当时最风行的几个小说家的批评——例如 Rebecca West，Romer Wilson，Hutchingson，Swinnerton，等——恐怕因为一般人不稔悉，那类简约的评语不能引起相当的兴味所以从略。麦雷自己是现在英国中年的评论家最有学有识的一人——他去年在牛津大学讲的 The Problem of Style[1]，有人誉为安诺德（Matthew Arnold）以后评论界最重要的一部贡献——而他总常常推尊曼殊斐尔，说她是评论的天才，有言必中肯的本能，所以我此刻要把她那晚随兴月且的珠沫，略过不讲，很觉得有些可惜。她说她方才从瑞士回来，在那里和罗素夫妇寓所相距颇近，常常说

_____

　　① 风格的问题。

起东方的好处，所以她原来对中国景仰，更一进而为爱慕的热忱。她说她最爱读 Arthur Waley 所翻的中国诗，她说那样的艺术在西方真是一个 wonderful revelation①，她说新近 Amy Lowell 译得很使她失望，她这里又用她爱用的短句 that's not the thing!② 她问我译过没有，她再三劝我应当试试，她以为中国诗只有中国人能译得好的。

她又问我是否也是写小说的，她又问中国顶喜欢契诃甫的哪几篇，译得怎么样，此外谁最有影响。

她问我最喜欢读哪几家小说，我说哈代，康德拉，她的眉稍耸了一耸笑道：

"Isn't it! We have to go back to the old masters for good literature——the real thing!" ③

她问我回中国去打算怎么样，她希望我不进政治，她愤愤地说现代政治的世界，不论哪一国，只是一乱堆的残暴和罪恶。

---

① 奇妙的启示。
② 不是那么回事！
③ "不是吗？我们必须从过去的大师那里寻找好文学——真东西！"

后来说起她自己的著作。我说她的太是纯粹的艺术，恐怕一般人反而不认识，她说：

"That's just it，then of course，popularity is never the thing for us." [1]

我说我以后也许有机会试翻她的小说，愿意先得作者本人的许可。她很高兴地说她当然愿意，就怕她的著作不值得翻译的劳力。

她盼望我早日回欧州，将来如到瑞士再去找她，她说怎样地爱瑞士风景，琴妮湖怎样的妩媚，我那时就仿佛在湖心柔波间与她荡舟玩景。

Clear，placid Leman！

……

Thy soft murmuring sounds sweet as if a

sister's voice reproved.

That I with stern delights should ever have

been so moved… [2]

---

[1] "确实，当然了，流行向来与我们无关。"

[2] "清澈、平静的莱蒙湖！……/你轻声低语，/似姐妹间责备般甜蜜，/让我体验未曾经历的感动和愉悦。"《恰尔德·哈罗德游记》，拜伦。

　　我当时就满口地答应，说将来回欧一定到瑞士去访她。

　　末了我恐怕她已经倦了，深恨与她相见之晚，但盼望将来还有再见的机会。她送我到房门口，与我很诚挚地握别。

　　将近一月前我得到曼殊斐尔已经在法国的芳丹卜罗①去世。这一篇文字，我早已想写出来，但始终为笔懒，延到如今，岂知如今却变了她的祭文了！

　　———————————

　　① 通译枫丹白露。